ENDORSEMENTS

When I think of authenticity, I think of David Winston. He courageously embraces his God-given purpose while simultaneously honoring the legacy of those who have come before him. In this book, you will not only read the intimate details of David's journey, but you'll also learn how to bravely forge your own path forward.

SAMUEL RODRIGUEZ
Senior Pastor of New Season Church
Sacramento, CA

If you are looking for encouragement, strength, and assurance that God's power is always at work within you, *Authentic* is a must-have.

KEL MITCHELL
American Actor and Stand-up Comedian

In *Authentic,* Pastor David Winston has put his finger on our collective pulse. He can, by that simple measure, tell us the condition of our hearts, the functions of our vital organs, and our health in general. He is right in asserting that your *what you do* should flow out of *who you are.* Who before what! I wish I had read this book earlier in my life journey—but it's not too late. I'm learning and growing, and you can too.

SAM CHAND
Speaker, Author, Leadership Consultant,
and friend of David Winston

I'm excited for the world to experience the revelatory brilliance of David Winston. This timely message in his new book highlights the power of embracing your uniqueness and empowers readers with the courage necessary to be their greatest self — divinely endowed to show up powerfully in every circumstance. If you're looking to discover the best version of yourself and to be activated for undeniable impact and abundance — this book is for you.

TOURÉ ROBERTS
Best-selling Author, Entrepreneur and
Founder of One Church LA

David Winston is a prolific writer. I unequivocally believe anyone reading this book will experience a supernatural transformation that defies human comprehension. This book is a literary tour-de-force and a must-read by anyone who is in search of practical tools for living authentically and materials that will help them discover their identity.

DR. N. CINDY TRIMM
Best Selling Author, Life & Business Strategist

Pastor David Winston isn't simply part of the generation leading the world back to God; he's leading the charge. The unique word God has given him has made an impact on my life personally, and the wisdom he imparts in this book will bless you beyond measure. I highly recommend it.

GIANNO CALDWELL
Fox News Analyst

Walking in the shadow of a great man is equivalent to asking a tree to blossom in the shade. Although difficult, it's not impossible. The arbequina olive tree perfects beauty without the necessity of constant sun. David Winston is just that kind of leader, one who has blossomed in the shade of a giant on his way to becoming one himself.

KEION HENDERSON
Senior Pastor of The Lighthouse Church
Houston, TX

If there's anything we need to work on in this day and age, it's the gift of being authentic. I'm so excited for the world to embrace the message of authenticity. I've known David for some time, and I'm unsure if there's anybody who is more qualified to write this book. Here's to us embracing our true and authentic selves.

CHRIS DURSO
Author of *The Heist: How Grace Robs Us of Our Shame*

David Winston's new book *Authentic* is a much-needed message for the Body of Christ today. So many people have idolized others or coveted the gift or assignment on other people's lives and have failed to live from an authentic place. This book is a God-centered and practical guide for helping people to truly receive and recover their identity. David embodies the message of this book, and I'm confident that those who read it will finally mute the voice of insecurity and comparison in their mind. Grab a copy ASAP.

MANNY ARANGO
Pastor and Creator of ARMA Bible Courses

What an important book, *Authentic*. David skillfully tackles what I believe to be one of the most important and needed topics today: knowing and valuing who you are. *Authentic* not only helps you to recognize the masterpiece you are, but it also helps you to dream again, live again, and win again. This is a must-read.

MICHELLE FERGUSON
CEO, Author, Speaker, and Award Winning Flautist

David Winston is a true example of knowing who you are in a broken world. Living a life of authenticity, he has helped others discover their purpose. In reading this book, you will uncover your true value and unique gifts that God has given you to live out a successful life.

PAUL DAUGHERTY
Lead Pastor of Victory Church
Tulsa, OK

Authentic—there's no question this is what people are looking for when they encounter us. Are you who you say you are, and can you do what you say you can do? Authentic leadership is what's needed. Authentic love is what's desired. Authentic *you* is what my friend Pastor David Winston is framing beautifully in this work. I encourage you to read *Authentic* and then read it again, as I know the man and the message to be the same!

CHRIS ESTRADA
Executive Leader of Missions Me
Executive Director of Missions Me College

AUTHENTIC

THE **David S. Winston**
CONFIDENCE
TO BE YOURSELF,
AUTHENTIC THE
COURAGE
TO RELEASE YOUR
GREATNESS

Published by Harrison House Publishers
Shippensburg, PA 17257

ISBN 13 TP: 978-1-6675-0012-6
ISBN 13 eBook: 978-1-6675-0013-3
ISBN 13 HC: 978-1-6675-0018-8

For Worldwide Distribution, Printed in the U.S.A.
1 2 3 4 5 6 7 8 / 27 26 25 24 23

CONTENTS

FOREWORD

Authentic: The Confidence to be Yourself, the Courage to Release Your Greatness is biblically insightful and "real world" instructive. Based on David's own journey and his almost fourteen years of pastoral ministry, *Authentic* is written to help others find their unique voice and God-given greatness, and it does not disappoint.

I have witnessed firsthand David's personal journey to authenticity and purpose. His passion to help people discover their authentic self and to see the bigger picture of God's plan only grows. He is especially gifted in reaching the younger generation with this life-changing message.

David was brought up on the Word of God. His mother, Veronica, and I taught him to believe God for everything—from vacations to his first car—and to do everything with excellence as unto the Lord. Even when David began working for the ministry as a janitor in high school, he served with all of his heart, desiring to be a role model for others.

Interestingly, in his youth David never thought that he would find himself in full-time ministry. He went to undergraduate school at Oral Roberts University with the thought to attend medical school and become a doctor, but God had other plans.

Today, he serves as our ministry's youth pastor and the worldwide director of Bill Winston Ministries. His exemplary leadership of our ministry offices in the United States, Africa and Canada has been extremely fruitful. David understands authority, which I think is one of the biggest contributors to his success. He is under authority as my assistant and under authority to God as a believer.

Releasing your greatness takes courage. Like Joseph in the book of Genesis, you may be misunderstood, rejected by family or even betrayed by others before you arrive at the palace and your place of destiny. The journey, however, is well worth it, as David confirms in the pages of this book.

David has found himself, and through *Authentic: The Confidence to Be Yourself, the Courage to Release Your Greatness,* he skillfully engages the reader to find their true value and significance and to bless the world around them with their discovery.

BILL WINSTON

INTRODUCTION

Look at your hands; examine the lines, creases, and distinctive print. Throughout all of history, no one has ever had the same fingerprints. This is what it means to be original.

You have one thing in common with every other person. When you wake up in the morning, go to the bathroom, and look in the mirror, you see your own face staring back at you. It's the same face that you have always had. Whether you are young or more mature, that same person has been with you your entire life. It's you! Unfortunately, many people look in the mirror and don't like what they see. And many others start the day filled with remorse because they don't like who they are. The truth is, whether you like it or not, you cannot escape who you are.

Millions of people every day suffer from low self-esteem. They wonder, *Why am I here? Why am I like this?*

What could I possibly have to offer? Feelings of inadequacy and inferiority fill their minds even before their first cup of coffee. This happens because people have not discovered the value they hold.

Inside each one of us is a treasure waiting to be exposed. You might say, "But I don't feel very valuable." The fact that you don't see the treasure doesn't mean it doesn't exist. Oftentimes in adventure movies, when the main characters have set off on a journey to find a hidden treasure, they have to believe the treasure exists and that it is where the map says it is. That's called *faith*—believing in the existence of something even though you cannot prove it with your natural senses alone. Those who have set out on this adventure must have faith. Their faith may start to wane, however, if they focus on the thought that this treasure may not exist. If they lose their faith, they lose their motivation to discover what lies ahead.

Fortunately, in a lot of adventure movies, the characters take the leap of faith, avoid death one or more times, and—spoiler alert—find the hidden treasure. Those movies show us that many of the most valuable treasures will take some work to discover and some faith for the journey. But once the treasure is revealed, the journey is always worth the work.

The great news is, I can tell you where the treasure is. The treasure is inside you! You hold something special, and many people are searching for it. It's your ability, talent, skill, and innate genius. The package that the treasure is placed in is your unique personality. The purpose of this book is to expose who you are, the real you, the treasure. The simple yet profound truths in this book will lead you on a spiritual journey of self-discovery that will transform your perspective. You will discover how to identify your uniqueness and how to value what God has put inside you. Instead of seeing your unique traits as liabilities to your success, you will now see where your abilities lie.

Do you ever get the sense that you are being prepared for something greater? Something more significant? Something that makes a greater impact on the world than what you are currently doing? I've been there—the nagging sense that there is more, followed by the longing feeling of curiosity. I would ask God, "How do I get to the *more?*" Soon I found that I was asking the wrong question. The question I needed to be asking was, "How do I *become* the *more?*" Instead of looking outside for opportunities, connections, and promotions, I started to look inside at my personality, passions, and proclivities.

Many are in search of purpose, but they are searching out of order. I've discovered that if you become who God has created you to be—your authentic self—purpose will actually start to find you. You hold the key.

The good news is, you don't have to change who you are to be significant.

In Authentic: The Confidence to Be Yourself, the Courage to Release Your Greatness, we will explore how to:

- Develop a positive self-image
- Understand your value
- Be confident in your uniqueness
- Identify personal limitations
- Determine your code of authenticity
- Avoid comparison pitfalls
- Find happiness in being you
- Discover your hidden abilities (potential)
- Choose the right environments
- Find courage in transparency

In each of these areas, you will find practical insights along with simple examples for interpersonal success. You will win in life by being yourself. It can be one of the easiest things to do while simultaneously being one of the hardest things to do. You may have never considered yourself as someone great or significant before now, but all of that is about to change. By following the principles and simple exercises in *Authentic*, you will find a new level of confidence and fulfillment, starting today.

Every person on earth has a God-given gift. Every gift comes with a built-in audience. This means that people are looking for what you carry and may not even be aware that you are carrying it. They might not be aware that they need what you have, but they do. When you present your gift, or the treasure that you carry, they will recognize their need for it. Thirty years ago no one thought they needed an Uber ride, a smartphone device, or a social media account. But the fact is, they didn't know they needed it until they were properly presented with the option to have it and discovered the value such innovations could add.

In this book, I will challenge you to leave the low self-image behind and forge a new path—a path of authenticity and significance. To understand your authentic purpose, you must understand the authentic you. You can only achieve what God has purposed for you to achieve by becoming who God has called you to be. Your code of authenticity is the secret to unshakeable confidence and the key to living a life of significance and impact.

It's time to stop behaving as if you have a personality impediment. You have been carefully crafted for this moment in history. You are God's chosen problem-solver, solution-bearer, and change advocate for this time. You have what this generation is looking for, even if you don't know it. Part of my purpose is to help you access what God has put inside of you so that you can change the fabric of society. You will be a history-maker and a game-changer. Something will come out of you, as a result of this new thinking, that will astound others. It's time to take hold of the future and discover who you really are.

CHAPTER 1

YOU CAN ONLY GO AS FAR AS YOUR WORTH

It was a Thursday in the spring of 2016. We were four weeks into our social emotional learning program. I was standing at the front of a vacant classroom next to the chalkboard. It was my turn to lead the weekly session with the students. I had my notes ready, but I was nervous. *Will they think this is stupid? I hope this goes well...* I thought to myself. *What happens if there is a fight among the students? Will we have to stop for the entire day?* These were the kind of opportunities we had been praying for. I was hopeful but anxious. But I took solace in knowing that I wasn't alone. Several youth leaders from our Go Hard for Christ youth ministry, a couple staff, and my wife Niki joined me. Little did I know that the conversation I was about to engage in with one particular teenager would change me forever.

Allow me to give you some context. We were at the Austin College and Career Academy, a public high school located in the Austin neighborhood, one of the most violent neighborhoods on the west side of Chicago. Things during that school year had been tough. The student morale at the school had dropped to an all-time low, with school attendance plunging, graduation rates sinking, violence surging, and parental involvement all but invisible. The staff were desperate for help. Something. Anything to stop the downward spiral.

That's when one of the staff at the high school, who also happened to be a member of our church, reached out to us at the start of the second semester to see if anything could be done. It was a great opportunity, and we immediately jumped at the chance to impact young lives. We just needed to figure out what to do and how exactly to do it. We knew it could be tricky walking the line between teaching biblical principles and proselytizing teenagers, which the administration said we were strictly prohibited from doing. Knowing that the program could serve as a launching pad to other godly initiatives in the school, the pressure was on to get this right. We understood the assignment and began praying for wisdom.

As a result of those prayers, we created a social emotional learning (SEL) program to help teens heal from the trauma they had experienced. As we started to implement the program the Lord gave us, we began seeing results. We were now four weeks into the program. I had just finished leading a session on the importance of forgiveness. Now it was time for these students to take action and forgive their offenders. Some of the girls were compliant, but unsurprisingly many of the guys were reluctant. So I did what good youth pastors do; I went to them.

I approached a sixteen-year-old young man who looked like he couldn't care less about our message or the forgiveness exercise. The teachers had warned me that he was a bit of a troublemaker and had a reputation for fighting in class. But that didn't scare me; I knew the root of his aggression came from pain. So I began to engage him with a few questions and some small talk.

I asked him, "So, after hearing this today, do you have anyone that you need to forgive?"

He looked at me, repulsed, and said, "Why would you expect me to forgive them?"

I reiterated some things I had said during the session and answered his questions while trying not to be too pushy. He quickly retaliated with frustration in his voice. He told me how his dad had been gone for years and made him feel like a mistake and burden. His mother was gone for days, even weeks at a time, often choosing drugs over being a parent. He said she claimed to keep him around for a government check, which she would use to buy drugs, basically saying she didn't care about him or his wellbeing as her child.

Suddenly, with tears in his eyes, he said one of the most gripping things I have ever heard a teenager say, "I am nothing. That's what they think, and that's what I am. I might as well die. They don't matter, and neither do I, so why forgive them?"

I would like to tell you that I said something divinely inspired at that moment, but that would be a lie. The truth is, I froze. I was speechless. I had no reply for what he said to me. We were there because we loved and valued the students. I knew our mission was to foster healing and deliver hope, but at that moment I just couldn't get the words out. What he said shook me to the core. I could tell other students felt the same way as they looked on with subtle nods of agreement. He said it loud enough that most of class could hear. After those students left, I just sat in the chair fighting back tears. I have never had to live his life, but I felt his pain. I felt compassion. I could only imagine what it would feel like to live life as if you didn't matter to anyone—to feel like nothing all the time. To exist void of value.

At that moment I had a revelation: This is what I was born to change. God reminds us in the scriptures, "Though my father and mother forsake me, the Lord will receive me" (Ps. 27:10 NIV). This is God's promise to us, but so many people today do not experience this reality. They live with low self-esteem, doubting their own worth. And God longs to reach their hearts with His truth. He longs to show them how valuable they are. *That day I discovered that one of the most important things missing in the hearts of humanity today is value.* People need to understand their value. And they need someone to help them discover it.

Everyone wants to feel significant. People pay thousands and thousands of dollars to get it. Some try to alter their appearance to increase their sense of value. Some join gangs to try to find it through a feeling of family. Others are quick to tell you their job title or credentials, assuming that will inflate their value in the eyes of the hearers. Many times people are just looking to feel significant. However, true value cannot be artificially manufactured. True and lasting value comes from within.

The conversation I had that day with that sixteen-year-old young man showed me what it was like to interact with someone who thought they had absolutely no value. I saw what was missing in the hearts of youth in the violence-stricken neighborhoods of Chicago. But in a system and society that is designed to strip you of it, value is hard to find. Flashing guns and money on social media is a counterfeit way of establishing value or significance. Upon this revelation, I identified three main points of emphasis by which we would help youth grow into better people: healing, value, and purpose. Purpose is simply the original reason for the existence of a thing—the reason why something was created. We believed working in those key areas would help kids see a better way and refuse to default to violent behavior. They would see themselves in a better light. They would value their decisions because they value themselves.

Everyone needs to feel like they have something to offer the world. One kid can shoot another kid because of this simple principle: When I don't value my life, I absolutely won't value yours. Youth need to see hope and a future so they can value the gift of life again. We can't let the circumstances we see around us determine the value of what's inside us.

WE ALL HAVE VALUE

This revelation isn't just for inner-city youth. It's for everyone. Value doesn't have borders or socioeconomic boundaries; we are all looking to feel valued. The pursuit of it may look different for teens living on the west or south side of Chicago compared to a middle-aged executive living in Manhattan. But the end goal is still finding significance. Value is the foundation on which the rest of this book is built. This journey that you will take is about understanding your unique value and what you bring to the world.

The earth has no back door. You cannot sneak into existence. You may have been born into less-than-ideal conditions, but that does not negate the fact that you were a calculated decision by God. Hearing these words alone should up the ante on your perception of your value.

VALUE LEADS TO DISCOVERY

Despite the fact that I was helping youth see their significance, I had been struggling with my own value. I had been feeling the weight of being compared to what my father, Dr. Bill Winston, has done in ministry. I wondered if I could live up to his example. As I was praying one day, God spoke to me. His words changed my outlook forever. He said to me, "You can't be everything that I have called you to be while trying to be someone else. You can't achieve what I have called you to achieve while trying to be someone else. You can't reach the people I have planned for you to reach if you don't become the only person I designed you to be: *you*."

From that moment forward, I discovered that my personality is *perfectly* suited for my purpose. My gift or ability is a unique asset that no one has ever seen before. My dad and I are both pastors and leaders, but what makes us unique is our personalities. Our unique personalities make us original. Originals have great value. God's words to me inspired me, and I decided I would not let my dad's success intimidate me anymore. We all have our own genre of success waiting to be uncovered.

The Bible says, "…Honestly assess your worth by using your God-given faith as the standard of measurement, and then you will see your true value with an appropriate self-esteem" (Rom. 12:3 TPT). If you don't think you are worth much, you will never let people see the real you. You can spend years hiding behind masks, pretending to be someone you're not, simply because you have a predetermined belief that others won't like you for you. Before they reject you, you have already rejected yourself. Let's take a moment to discover where we derive our value.

WHERE VALUE COMES FROM

Value can simply be defined as our personal appraisal of ourselves. Value is our internal self-worth. It's our self-assessment, the story our mind tells our heart, and what we say about ourselves. Value is the glue that holds our self-esteem together. If you have no value, your self-esteem is bound to fall apart. *Value* can also be defined as the usefulness of something. When something is useful, it is needed, and its value cannot be called into question. So the real question is, what and who are influencing your *perceived* value?

Let me share a story first. When my wife Niki and I first got married, we had a lot of adjustments to make.

I was not just marrying her, but I also became a step-father to two amazing boys, Jacob and Jordan. Jacob, our oldest son, is a fun-loving guy who's always full of energy and laughter. One day, a few months into our marriage, something interesting happened. We noticed that Jacob had been acting distant for a few days, which was out of character for him. Niki asked him if everything was okay, and Jacob finally started to open up. He said, "Dad called me dumb." Niki looked at me as my jaw dropped. I said I would never do something like that, because I know how damaging those words can be. In fact, Jacob is a very smart young man. I immediately asked for more clarity, because I couldn't remember saying anything like that to him.

After a series of questions, we finally got to the root of it. Earlier that week, Jacob got caught doing something mischievous, and I felt like he was trying to act clueless about what he had done (even though he was aware of what had happened). At the time I said to him, "Don't act dumb." Of course, I would never imply that anyone's child is dumb, especially my own. I was just using it as a figure of speech, meaning stop pretending like you don't know what you did. Looking back, I can see that it was a poor choice of words, because that's not how he heard what I said. Once I identified the issue, I quickly apologized and said I never meant for those words to be a personal insult toward him. I explained that it was a figure of speech, but one that I will not use again. At that moment, I discovered how much power the words of others have in shaping one's value, especially when you are young. What I said was different than what he heard, but he was still emotionally paralyzed for those few days.

What other people express about you can have a strong impact on how you feel about yourself. However, your opinion can still have the most powerful influence on your sense of value. What you say and think about yourself carries more weight than anything that anyone else will say about you.

People will say things about you that you might not like. That's a fact of life. But you still get to choose what you believe about yourself. When you know that what they said is not true, then you won't repeat it. When you are not sure, you might consider it more and even repeat it to yourself. If what someone says about you confirms a preexisting bias or internal struggle, you may be likely to adopt it as a confirmation of your negative suspicions. That's when negative opinions become most poisonous to your value and self-worth.

T. D. Jakes said it like this, "If you are standing in a room full of people, you can see everyone else. The only person that you can't see is yourself."[1] This means you must depend on others to be a mirror for you, to give you an accurate reflection of who you are and what you look like. But what if they speak negatively to you and about you? Then it is likely that you will think negatively about yourself. If all the people close to you devalue you, how can you feel good about yourself?

Many different things, people, and situations can play a role in determining our self-image. Here are **eight influences** that I have found to be the most common in **shaping our value:**

1. **Teachers, parents, family members, spouses, authority figures, and friends** hold a tremendous amount of weight in our minds and hearts. Often, the closer they are to us the more damage their opinion can do to us. In the same respect, their words used the right way can have a tremendous ability to build us up.

2. **The environments in which we live or grow up in can influence us.** Some who come from low-income neighborhoods can feel low about themselves because that's what they see around them. Broken environments can often work to produce a broken self-image inside of us.

3. **Faults and failures** can work as slow cancers, eating away at our self-image. The reminders of our past and constant replays of our failures try to convince us that we are not as strong, good, or talented as we think.

4. **Lack of opportunities** can make us feel devalued, like we don't have that much to offer.

5. Many times we can derive value from our **romantic relationships.** However, when we have no meaningful relationships in our lives, this lack can cause us to feel devalued because we feel unloved.

6. **Abusive situations**, especially domestic abuse, often make the victims feel less valuable. They leave feeling like they have little or no significance at all, like they have nothing to offer the world. The internal damage of long-term abuse can be devastating.

7. **Money, possessions, and positions of power** can be among the most common things that people based their value on. The lack of it can have a negative impact on one's value.

8. **Social media** has come on strong in the last decade. It has its benefits, but it also has its challenges. Unfortunately, it has become a breeding ground for unhealthy comparison. Much of what is posted is filtered, edited, and fabricated. It allows you to see the highlights of others lives while concealing their challenges, mistakes, and disappointments. All too often this can leave you with the overwhelming sensation that you are not doing enough. Like you are not enough.

SEEING THE RIGHT WAY

Let's be honest: You can never escape yourself. You can change your name, dye your hair, or move to a different town, but you will still be you everywhere you go. If your desire in life is to become someone you're not, you will live in constant disappointment. If that sounds like you, I have good news. This no longer has to be your story.

It's true that life can throw us some curveballs. Things aren't always easy to figure out. At times, just when we thought we had it all figured out, life has an interesting way of humbling us. But as we keep our faith, hope, and trust in God, we will see His ultimate plan unfold in our lives. Robert Schuller wrote a book on this very topic, and the title says it all: *Tough Times Never Last, But Tough People Do.*

I was blessed to have a good family with two parents who loved me and provided for me, but I still experienced my own set of disappointments. At times, those disappointments tried to convince me that I am not as good as I think. But when you know who you are, your value stays intact, and you can go through disappointments without becoming damaged. The Bible says, "For as he thinks in his heart, so is he..." (Prov. 23:7 AMP). This means you will live life according to who you think you are.

Value can be relative according to the person assessing the value. The value of a cold gallon of water may be far higher to someone dying of thirst in the Sahara Desert than to a person who owns a water well in the Amazon rain forest. As the old saying goes, beauty is in the eye of the beholder. Perceived value and real value can be two different things. If you look to those around you to correctly assess your value, they may leave you feeling devalued. However, your value cannot be dictated by those who did not create you. Your value can only be *properly* assessed by the one who has been given the right and proper authority to dictate value. The only one who can define your value to the world is the great Creator, God.

VALUE: THE GATEWAY TO GREATNESS

Value unlocks courage because it gives you the strength to try hard things. Value unlocks performance because with it you believe you can do better. Value makes you a better leader because it makes you more secure. Instead of competing with people, you will work to complete people by helping them better their deficiencies. Value makes you a better friend because you will not be jealous of the successes of others. Instead, you will celebrate them. Value makes you a better person because it causes you to notice the value in others. Adding value to others is how we exercise our own unique greatness.

I can remember back to the very first sermon I preached to the whole congregation of our church, Living Word Christian Center (in Forest Park, Illinois). It was about a year after I had become the pastor of our youth ministry. I remember exactly where I was when I got the invitation via phone call. I was standing in the toy aisle of a Target store when my phone rang. It was my dad, so of course I answered the call. "David, I want you to bring the word at Wednesday night Bible study next week while I am out." Immediately, I started thinking of every excuse for why I could not or should not do it, but Dad was not having any of it. He would not accept excuses, and he took authority over the spirit of fear. He encouraged me and told me that I have a word from the Lord. I gave excuses and tried to pass up this wonderful opportunity because I didn't value what I carried, at least not yet. I didn't think the message I would give would be very powerful. I didn't think I had what it took to do the job well. And I didn't think people would want to hear any revelations that God had given me.

Boy, was I wrong! I delivered that message, and people were so blessed by it that they still mention it to me over a decade later. It taught me this important lesson: You should never undervalue what you carry. If you do, you could miss out on some divine opportunities that God set up just for you.

Value is what this book is all about. You must value yourself. No one else can do it for you. You need to know your value just as much as the sixteen-year-old boy on the west side of Chicago. You were not born to be thrown away. You weren't

> **God designed us to thrive when we know the value we carry.**

designed to be useless. You can and will be used by God to do something great in this life—not great according to human metrics, but great according to God's divine metrics. No one can do the job of valuing you *for* you. Your value starts with what you say and what you think.

We all have a destiny that God has assigned to us, but we won't even attempt the journey if we don't think we are good enough to walk down the road. The strength lies in knowing that you are the only one who can.

EXERCISE: GROWING YOUR VALUE

From this moment forward, start telling yourself a different story. You will reproduce in your life the thoughts you meditate on. As you meditate on this scripture below, your thoughts about yourself will begin to change. As you speak this scripture, you are legislating your future, giving the Word of God authority to make this a reality in your life.

1. Say this scripture below out loud seven times a day, every day, for ninety days:

    I will praise You, for I am fearfully and wonderfully made; marvelous are Your works, and that my soul knows very well (Psalm 139:14).

2. Every time you are tempted to complain about yourself, say something positive about yourself instead.

CHAPTER 2

THE PECULIAR PACKAGE

I'd be willing to guess that you have bought something online in the last few weeks. It might have been some new shoes, a birthday present for a loved one, or even this book. We all know that online shopping has become extremely popular over the last decade. Long gone are the days of waiting in endless lines during the Christmas shopping season. Thank God, because that easily makes my top ten list of all time least favorite things to do, right next to pulling weeds.

Fortunately, you can order just about anything online and get it shipped to your house in the next couple of days without any hassle. Our family will often order things online. I'm convinced that my wife has invested in Amazon stock the way she orders those packages. My kids always get excited when they see a package at the door (almost daily), even when it's not for them. Usually, the bigger the package, the more interested they are in opening it. One thing is for sure, we all like the feeling of receiving something meaningful.

At our church, Living Word Christian Center, we love to give to others. Every year, we give away prizes at our New Year's Eve service. The reason for the service is to celebrate the year as a church family and give thanks to God for another year of blessings. On one particular year, every person who came to the service received a festive, colored wristband before they got to their seat. When it was time to give out prizes, we chose a color and asked the person wearing that color wristband to come up and receive their gift. During a service a few years back, I had the opportunity to call some of the prizewinners to the stage for their gifts.

For the second prize drawing, I called for the winner wearing the white wristband to come up to the stage to claim the prize, but no one responded. Everyone looked around in anticipation for ten seconds...twenty seconds...still no one walked up. In my earpiece, I heard our event coordinator telling me to move on, but something told me that someone had that white wristband. Since no one had come up, we had to move forward. As some might know, my dad does not like to hold up the service.

About forty-five minutes later, the ushers told me they had found the winner with the white wristband. That night he was serving on one of our volunteer teams and assisting people outside. I was excited to give the prize to one of our faithful volunteers and even more excited when he told me what he had been doing outside. As he was serving that night, he was making sure that everyone who came received a wristband. As he distributed the wristbands, one woman received a white wristband. She commented that she thought it was defective, because it wasn't brightly colored. She gave it back to him, and he gave her a different one. He decided to take that unwanted wristband as his wristband. Everyone went on about their business until the moment when the white wristband was called up during the prize drawing.

When word finally reached him that no one seemed to have the white wristband, he suddenly remembered the one he had taken from the woman earlier. For the sake of time, he had put it into his pocket. Within the hour, I called him back onto the stage to claim his prize. The prize he won was a new 55-inch 4K curved flatscreen TV with an entertainment sound system. He stood there looking at me with a look of amazement and genuine shock. But he didn't win that prize by coincidence. I found out a few weeks later that he had been praying, asking God for a new TV in time to host a Super Bowl party. His prayers were answered!

Later, I discovered what the woman had said to him. She didn't know she had the winning wristband in her hand. Even though the back of every wristband was white, only the front of one wristband was white. She thought the white wristband was a defect, but it turned out to be the most special of all. She gave it away without knowing the value it carried.

Can you relate to being rejected because you are unique in a way that seems awkward? Have you looked at certain characteristics about yourself and marked them as defects? Do you feel like you have been overlooked, put back on the shelf, or hidden in someone's pocket? The fact is, if you don't know your worth, you will always sell yourself short. But the good news is, God doesn't see you that way. He inspired David to write these words of truth that apply to you "…I am fearfully and wonderfully made…" (Ps. 139:14).

Often, what you may see as differences and defects are markings from the Creator to remind you that you have been personally crafted and chosen by Him. *You may have thought your difference was a mistake, but I'm here to tell you that it's a gift.* The volunteer's prize was exactly what he needed right when he needed it—made possible by a so-called defective wristband. The wristband was only perceived to be defective because it was different; in reality, it was special. Friend, let me tell you that your difference, your unique personality, and what you carry are all very significant. The scripture says, "He has made everything beautiful in its time…" (Eccl.

3:11). It's possible that others won't notice or understand your significance, but don't worry. Your significance is not up to them; it's up to Him—our Creator. In time they will see you blossom like a beautiful flower. Let me take a moment to tell you my story about discovering my own significance.

DISCOVERING MY SIGNIFICANCE

For many years people have asked me, "How does it feel to be Bill Winston's son and have to follow in his steps and walk in his shoes?"

Growing up, my response was usually something like, "I don't really know. I've never known life as someone else. It's good I guess, but a little intimidating. However, I just don't know anything different."

Now, years later, as an adult and father myself, I see how incredibly blessed I am to have a father as great as my dad. From every moment playing tennis on the tennis courts to having morning Bible study at the dining room table, he poured into me in a way that I cannot describe with words. It's because of him that I am the man I am today.

Growing up in ministry, I had a front-row seat to see God do many amazing things. In 1988, my family came to Chicago with $200 and no place to live. My parents made the move in obedience, because God told them to start a church in Chicago. God moved on a woman's heart to allow us to stay with her for several months (free of charge) until we could get on our feet. Mom and Dad didn't have a lot of money, but they did have a lot of faith. Our first official church building was a small storefront location on the west side of Chicago in one of the highest crime neighborhoods of the city at that time. That building was barely the size of a school classroom.

From there, because of their trust in God, over the last three decades our ministry has grown to become a worldwide church ministry, creating hundreds of jobs, starting the nationally accredited Joseph Business School, and gaining major influence in our city. Our church now owns multiple mall properties that have many stores in them, yet still none are as small as the storefront space we started in. In fact, at the time of the writing of this book, Dad is still the senior pastor of LWCC and very actively engaged in growing and developing the ministry. To say that I have seen God use my father to do incredible things would be an understatement.

None of those achievements or accomplishments used to intimidate me…until God put it on my heart to go into full-time ministry. Prior to that, I had planned on going into the medical field (I will share more on that later). All my life, people had asked me if I was going to be a pastor like my dad, and I would confidently say, "Nope!" But in retrospect, I think I was more fearful than anything. Once I went into full-time ministry in 2009, I would start to wonder about how I was going to step up and do something like what Dad had done. The bigger question was: *Do I even have what it takes to be great? Will what I have be enough for the people I'm supposed to lead?* These questions bothered me for the first several years in ministry. Few truly understood, and even fewer knew about the process God was taking me through to purge my insecurities.

Then, one morning in prayer, as doubt and insecurity were trying to get the best of me, I heard God's voice in the midst of my own chaotic thoughts. His voice said, "You could never fulfill the purpose that your dad was called to fulfill."

At that moment, I was thinking, *Yes, of course. God, we both know I couldn't do what my dad was called to do during the time he was called to do it.* It's wasn't the sudden jolt of divine confidence I had hoped for.

But what He said next was the part that completely shifted my paradigm. God said, "And your dad could never fulfill what you are about to do."

WAIT! Stop the tape. Rewind...what?? It was like something exploded inside of me. I had never thought about it like that. Hearing this was like music to my ears. What was once intimidating was now intriguing to me. Even the thought that I could do something that my father possibly could not do was amazing to me. The more I meditated on this thought, the more insight came. I discovered that I had been putting false expectations on myself. And the only expectations that I have to measure up to are the ones God has for me. I had been focusing so much on what I *was not* that I had abandoned what I *was*. I had neglected to pay attention to my own pedigree of genius.

We all have our own pedigree of genius. Sometimes we look at prominent people we respect and think about how we could never do what they have done. But if you flip the story around, you will realize that they are not equipped to do what you can do either. As gifted as they are, they can't do what you can do. Don't focus on who you are not. Focusing on who you are not will always leave you regretting who you are. Your very existence highlights God's creative genius, bringing glory to Him. If God is proud of His creation, you should be too.

I can't do everything my dad can do and has done. As much as I love, respect, and honor my father, as well as value what he's taught me, the truth is, he can't do what I'm called to do, because he doesn't have what God gave me. God gave me my personality as my gift. My difference maker. It's the vehicle He wants to use to get the attention of others. In fact, God is counting on our differences to further facilitate the accomplishment of His will. Both of us are absolutely necessary even though we are different.

DIFFERENT PARTS, EQUAL VALUE

The apostle Paul writes about us being different parts of the same body as followers of Christ:

> *The human body has many parts, but the many parts make up one whole body. So it is with the body of Christ...we have all been baptized into one body, by one Spirit, and we all share the same Spirit. Yes, the body has many different parts, not just one part. If the foot says, "I am not a part of the body because I am not a hand," that does not make it any less a part of the body. And if the ear says, "I am not part of the body because I am not an eye," would that make it any less a part of the body? If the whole body were an eye, how would you hear? Or if your whole body were an ear, how would you smell anything? But our bodies have many parts, and God has put each part just where he wants it* (1 Corinthians 12:12–18 NLT).

In the Body of Christ, we are called to come together as one. We are assigned to be the perfect complement to each other for the common goal of advancing the Kingdom of God. That means that we are not competing with each other; we are completing each other. We all represent different parts, meaning that we have different skills, personalities, and abilities. We are all valuable. Yes, that means you!

We know that every part of our human body is necessary. Even two parts that may seem similar in function are both still necessary. You wouldn't get rid of one hand because you have two. That would make everyday tasks much harder. It's much easier to type a text message with two thumbs! Health professionals say that if you didn't have your big toe on your foot you wouldn't be able to walk upright. You can't balance your weight properly without your big toe. As small and seemingly insignificant as it is, it's a necessary part. It's not an elbow. It's not an ear. It's not a finger. Your toe is not even always visible. But if it is missing, multiple other parts of your body are adversely affected. Every part is worthy of its place.

Not everyone is designed to do what you are doing or are going to do. Many people are not designed to do what I'm doing, and that's OK. I like to read this scripture passage from 1 Corinthians 12 frequently, because it reminds me that we are all necessary and uniquely indispensable. My father and I could function independently of one another in ministry, doing the work of the Lord, but we are better together. However, we couldn't accomplish as much collectively if we didn't allow our individual natural abilities and talents to shine through.

My wife and I have four kids all together, and all of them have completely different personalities even though they have mostly grown up in the same household. This is because their life purposes requires them to be unique. Your purpose requires you to be unique too. We are all designed to be different, just like the keys of a piano. God made it that way so we can all work in concert together to produce something beautiful, just like the piano that produces harmonious sounds. It can only make beautiful music when all of the keys are unique.

PERSONALITY IS YOUR WRAPPING PAPER

God made you unique because the needs of the people all over the world are unique. Your purpose in life will ultimately affect other people. But it's not just about what you do; it's about who you are. *Who you are is what attracts them to what you carry.* And what you carry is a valuable gift.

Imagine that I'm about to give you a present. I have two very similar items in two identical white boxes. One of the boxes is wrapped in blue gift-wrapping paper, and the other one is wrapped in red paper. When I give these wrapped gifts to you, I tell you to choose only one. You don't know what's in the box, because you can only see the outside. Now if red is your favorite color, you might be more likely to pick the one wrapped in red wrapping paper. On the other hand, just because the gift with blue wrapping paper was not picked doesn't mean something was wrong with that gift. You are just more likely to choose according to your preference. Do you see how the presentation of the package mattered? It's the same way with the personalities that God has given us. This is one of the most important statements that I will make in this book: Your personality is how God packages your gift and presents it to the world.

Personalities are what make us unique, even when we feel like our gift is similar to someone else's gift. It's who you are that determines how your gift is delivered to the world. Just like you have a favorite color or smell, *you are someone's favorite expression of the ability that you carry.* The fact that the red gift was preferred had more to do with the recipient than the actual content of the gift. Remember, God will take you to a people, place, and environment where they prefer your gift delivered to them through your personality, because that's the way they will receive it best. Say this out loud, "I am someone's favorite person for the job!"

> **"**
> **Your personality is how God packages your gift and presents it to the world.**
> **"**

You can't enter into the destiny that God has for you trying to be someone else. Let's recall what David said in the book of Psalms, "Thank you for making me so wonderfully complex! Your workmanship is marvelous—how well I know it" (Ps. 139:14 NLT). God has made us marvelous and wonderfully complex—all of us. Some of us are a little more complex than others, and some like things much simpler. You are a marvel (even though you might not be a superhero). That is not just for those who come from a good neighborhood, went to college, live in a nice house, are physically fit, or have the right connections. This is true for every single person, without exception. Don't question how you are made. God doesn't make accidents. He has never made an accident in the history of the universe, and He didn't start with you. Nothing about you is accidental. You were carefully constructed, calculated, and designed.

HIS MASTERPIECE

> *For we are His workmanship [His own master work, a work of art], created in Christ Jesus [reborn from above–spiritually transformed, renewed, ready to be used] for good works, which God prepared [for us] beforehand [taking paths which He set], so that we would walk in them [living the good life which He prearranged and made ready for us]* (Ephesians 2:10 AMP).

In the book of Ephesians, the apostle Paul reminds us of who we really are and who made us. The word *workmanship* in the Greek is *pŏiēma,*[1] which is the origin of our English word *poem.* This word means "masterpiece or work of art." When I think of a masterpiece, I think of the famous painting *Mona Lisa* created by Leonardo da Vinci. The *Mona Lisa* is the best known, most visited, most written about, and most sung about work of art in the whole world.[2] The *Mona Lisa* is one-of-a-kind, but what makes it so great?

It is recorded that it took da Vinci 16 years to complete the painting of the *Mona Lisa*. Unlike other paintings of the 16th century, the Mona Lisa was a very realistic portrait of a real person. Contemporary art connoisseur Mariana Custodio had this to say about da Vinci:

> To create a masterpiece you have to be a master yourself. And Leonardo da Vinci was an absolute genius. Drawing, painting, sculpting, da Vinci was also an engineer, a scientist, an architect and a theorist—a man of many talents you may say.[3]

Many scholars consider the *Mona Lisa* a masterpiece because of the difficult techniques displayed in color blending and the subtle gradations of light and shadow to model form. Custodio goes on to say:

> Mona Lisa's softly sculpted face shows how innovative da Vinci was in regards to exploring new techniques... In addition to its incredible technicalities, the

woman's soft smile is incredibly alluring. There's also a thing called the Mona Lisa Effect: The resonance of her facial expression depends on the angle from which the viewer approaches it.[4]

Many scholars, however, point out that the excellent quality of the *Mona Lisa* alone was not enough by itself to make the painting a celebrity. There are, after all, many good paintings. Many external events also contributed to the artwork's fame, starting with the inclusion of the painting in the royal collection of Francis I, king of France. It remained in French palaces until the French Revolution claimed the royal collection as the property of the people. It then found its way into Napoleon's bedroom before being installed in the Louvre Museum at the turn of the ninteenth century.[5] And we know just how much rich and powerful people like to show off their art collections, especially a piece as significant as the *Mona Lisa*.

Consider everything that went into this painting: time, unparalleled attention to detail, innovative techniques, and a master creator's touch. All of these factors also went into your composition by the ultimate Creator, God. As He employed His divine tools, a masterpiece was born: you. God calls you His masterpiece— something that can't be duplicated, erased, or replaced. Ephesians 2:10 says you are God's work of art, even more valuable than da Vinci's famous painting. And you have been created at just the right time in history. You must trust that the great Creator produced the right creation for the right time. God is ready to show you off as one of His most prized pieces. You must have faith in yourself. After all, you're one of God's greatest creations.

Now, let me share a new revelation with you: Look closely at the *Mona Lisa*. Do you see her eyebrows? No, because she doesn't have any. Take a minute to look it up online. Isn't that strange? I've always wondered what the story is behind that. Maybe an eyebrow threading appointment gone horribly wrong. Maybe she was born with a condition of some kind. Regardless of the reason, here is my point: *Even a masterpiece has small defects or flaws, but people don't stop calling it a masterpiece.* These small defects didn't make people value the *Mona Lisa* any less. Those defects didn't stop people from visiting the painting, writing about it, or even singing about it.

> **You're not a masterpiece because you're flawless. You're a masterpiece because you are priceless.**

Maybe you have examined yourself and noticed that you have some flaws. So what? You're not a masterpiece because you're flawless. You're a masterpiece because you're priceless. You may have an awkward laugh, a few bumps, or a mental challenge. You might feel like you don't fit in because of your differences. Don't let some flaws stop you from living a full life. Don't let those flaws make you hide in isolation. Put yourself on display like the masterpiece you are. You are an original. Be true to yourself, allowing the world to see something they have never seen before. You are one of a kind. And you have eyebrows!

FLAWS ARE HIS ACCESS POINTS

In the Bible, Jeremiah was a young prophet for the nation of Israel. God called him at a young age, and sometimes Jeremiah didn't quite understand what God was doing. We see this in the following dialogue between God and Jeremiah:

> *"Before I formed you in the womb I knew you; before you were born I sanctified you; I ordained you a prophet to the nations."*
>
> *Then said I: "Ah, Lord God! Behold, I cannot speak, for I am a youth."*
>
> *But the Lord said to me: "Do not say, 'I am a youth,' For you shall go to all to whom I send you, and whatever I command you, you shall speak"* (Jeremiah 1:5–7).

In another translation it says, "*…I do not know how to speak…*" (Jer. 1:6 AMP), meaning that Jeremiah was not an eloquent speaker. However, God said that before He formed Jeremiah in the womb He knew him. Before you were formed in your mother's womb, God knew you. Do you know what that means? It means that He designed you with a specific personality on purpose. You weren't an experiment. He knows your weaknesses and your strengths.

God knew Jeremiah's personality and still ordained him as a prophet to the nations. God even knew of the things that Jeremiah would see as flaws. But what Jeremiah thought was a flaw, God used as an *access point* that would ultimately give Jeremiah more access to the power and grace of God through his dependence on Him.

Perhaps you have found yourself asking God why He didn't make you better at something or more perfect in an area. I believe He did this so we can learn to trust Him with our perceived deficiencies. These "flaws" in our personhood are designed to make us more dependent on God's ability. Perfection can breed pride, but imperfection can lead to humility. Our weaknesses create the need to become more dependent on God's wisdom, strength, and power.

When God started speaking, Jeremiah immediately gave some excuses as to why he could not speak. God, however, didn't seem to think his excuses mattered. Have you ever given God excuses before? I know

I have. It never seems to work. The truth is, God won't ask us to do something we are incapable of, especially when His power is available to us. God is a forgiver of sins, but He doesn't tolerate excuses. If He tells you to do it, you are then responsible for obeying Him, just like Jeremiah was.

The way Jeremiah overcame his fear of speaking was to listen to God, go where God told him to go, and say whatever God told him to say. In other words, he had to become totally dependent on God. If Jeremiah had gone where God didn't send him and said what God didn't say, then disobedience would have magnified Jeremiah's flaws. When we obey God, our flaws decrease in significance. When we disobey God, we unknowingly magnify our flaws. Doubting God leads us to doubt ourselves.

Whenever Jeremiah followed through on what God said, the anointing on his life made up for his personality flaws or defects. The anointing is the power of God that gives you access to unlimited possibilities. My dad likes to say it this way, "It's the power of God that comes on human flesh that empowers you to do what only God can do." You must listen to God and do what He says to do. Your pursuit of purpose will require you to trust God every step of the way. It's just that simple. The scripture says that we are to *"...walk by faith, not by sight"* (2 Cor. 5:7). *This journey of life will require more dependence on God, not less.*

I can relate to Jeremiah, because I had the same excuse. When God spoke to my heart to go into full-time ministry in 2007, I was so nervous. I was nervous because I was not a good public speaker, and I thought I did not have what it took to do what God was asking me to do. All I could see were my flaws. But what I found was that the more I trusted God and relied on His anointing, the less nervous I felt. The more I relied on His strength, the more my weakness faded away. His power made possible the things that I could not do before. Today, I speak to thousands and feel more comfortable than I ever thought I would. That's only because of the grace of God. And if He did it for me, He can do it for you!

NOT PERFECT, BUT PERFECTED

Recently, I read a book about the power of the Holy Spirit.[6] The author talks about submitting his weaknesses to the power of the Holy Spirit rather than justifying them with a personality type. He asks the Holy Spirit to help him with his flaws or things that he considers weaknesses. He mentions the apostle Paul's statement:

> But he answered me, "My grace is always more than enough for you, and my power finds its full expression through your weakness." So I will celebrate my weaknesses, for when I'm weak I sense more deeply the mighty power of Christ

living in me. So I'm not defeated by my weakness, but delighted! For when I feel my weakness and endure mistreatment—when I'm surrounded with troubles on every side and face persecution because of my love for Christ—I am made yet stronger. For my weakness becomes a portal to God's power (2 Corinthians 12:9–10 TPT).

This means you don't have to feel defeated or helpless when considering your flaws and weaknesses. You can submit them to the Holy Spirit, and He will help you refine yourself. He will help you get better. That's good news! He'll help you transform into the image of Christ. Instead of using your personality type as an excuse or justification for your weaknesses, submit them to the Lord for growth.

EXERCISE: CULTIVATING SIGNIFICANCE

Every day write something positive about yourself. You can write it down in a journal or type it in your notes on your smartphone. Here are some examples:

- I look really good today.
- I am a very creative thinker.
- People always seem to enjoy being around me because I make them laugh.
- I am excellent at being on time for things.

AUTHENTIC

- I exercise resilience really well.
- I am good at being there for people and encouraging others.

During times when you feel discouraged, go back and review your list to be reminded of your significance.

CHAPTER 3

JUST BE YOU AND WIN

Have you ever heard a word or phrase that hit home so much that it seemed like it was written on your heart in permanent marker? I have. The word was *strategist*. It was the one word that stood out to me the most from a prophetic word that a very well-known and well-respected prophet gave to me one year during our annual leadership conference. As I stood there pondering what had been spoken over me, I started to see why the word *strategist* struck me as significant.

Allow me to give you some back story. For years, I struggled with feeling that I was a negative person. I could never figure it out, because I am naturally an encourager. I love to encourage people any time I have the chance. Because of this, I didn't label myself as a pessimist, but I did tend to easily see potential problems or, more specifically, the way plans *wouldn't* work. It came quite naturally to me. But the way people around me often reacted caused me to constantly doubt myself. I would tell myself to be more positive, that everything would work out fine. But all too often I would feel guilty and faithless, as if what I saw lying ahead prompted me to not take a position of faith. This was a constant struggle for me. I often wondered, *God, why did You make me this way?* It was something that I could never quite figure out—until that night when I received that prophetic word.

MY LIABILITY TURNED INTO AN ASSET

As I continued to reflect on the prophetic word, I asked the Lord, "What does *strategist* mean, and why does it seem so significant to me?" The Lord began to remind me that He made me on purpose for a purpose. Then God began to shift my perspective so that I could get a better understanding of my purpose through my unique personality. I like to say that He began to pull back the curtain. He showed me that a strategist is someone skilled in planning and systematically applying solutions. The key word here is *solutions.* It was never about the problems, but about His solutions. The problems were just a pathway to help me discover His wisdom, to enable me to employ the right solutions for various systems, situations, and circumstances.

That day my perception changed. I discovered that God created me to more readily identify problems because He has gifted me to be a problem solver. You can't solve a problem that you don't know exists. Developing a solution is always dependent on identifying the problem first. But I had never considered that the one who can see the problem can also be the one who is gifted with the ability to solve the problem.

I quickly realized my error! *What I thought was a flaw was actually a gift in disguise.* No problem on earth is without a solution, but I have to go deeper into my relationship with God to access the divine wisdom I need. I discovered that I can create and give solutions. That simple divine insight into how I was made caused me to reconsider my self-perception. What I had imagined to be a liability was really just a lie about

> **"**
> **What I had imagined to be a liability was really just a lie about my ability.**
> **"**

my ability. The devil, who is full of lies, will often try to lie to you about who you are and what you are capable of. The scripture says that he is the father of lies, and there is no truth in him (see John 8:44). Maybe he has lied to you about your ability. But remember, the devil is not your creator. God is your Creator, and He is the only one who knows the full scope of your potential through the agency of your personality.

A good example of this is Mark Zuckerberg, the founder and co-creator of Facebook.[1] With almost three billion users to date, Facebook is one of the most widely used social media platforms ever built. But it all started because Zuckerberg identified a problem. He noticed that Google was great for searching the news, and Wikipedia was great for searching for reference material, but there was no platform for searching and learning about other people. The solution he created, which was prompted by identifying a specific problem, is now affecting billions of people around the world. That one solution changed his life and his wallet. We can see now that he was created with a gift to solve a specific problem, and that insight turned into one of the most lucrative solutions in modern history.

This is what is happening with many people today. They don't understand why they were created the way they were created, so their ignorance darkens their perception of themselves. I wrote this book to help you get a fresh perspective on your personality and a clear understanding of how you were created. Knowledge changes behavior. When you know who you are, you behave differently.

Perhaps people or situations in your past have made you feel like you are "too much" of this or "not enough" of that. Here are some common criticisms that you might be able to identify with:

- You're being too optimistic.
- You're too daring or careless.

- You have compulsive behaviors.
- You overthink things.
- You're too nice.
- You always treat everything like it's a joke. Not everything is funny.
- You're just so strong/bossy/controlling all the time.
- You're so serious all the time; lighten up.
- You're so happy all the time; chill.
- You are so nonchalant about everything. Nothing ever affects you.
- All you care about is school/work/your business. You are too driven.

It can be discouraging to hear these comments. It casts a continual shadow of doubt on our proclivities. However, each one of these traits can be a valuable asset when placed in the right circumstance. People who are unfazed by or nonchalant about what happens around them can be a great asset when working in emergency response. Others who find humor in life can create pockets of laughter in the midst of discouraging situations and give those who are struggling a jolt of happiness. Your temperament is valuable. The value just needs to be discovered.

Learning more about myself gave me more confidence in who I am and what I've been created to do. I believe that as you read this book, the same will happen for you. Remember, not everyone will understand you, but you don't have to change who you are to be desired. Of course, we should always look to improve ourselves,

> **Authenticity is always in high demand. Life's experiences help us realize our code of authenticity.**

but there is a difference between making improvements and being an imposter. You must be authentic. Authenticity is always in high demand. Life's experiences help us realize our code of authenticity.

GOD CHOSE THE RIGHT PERSON

Jesus reminded His disciples of this truth, "You did not choose me, but I chose you and appointed you that you should go and bear fruit and that your fruit should abide..." (John 15:16 ESV). Let's never get this confused: We didn't choose God. He chose us. Then He assigned us a purpose. You did not pick out your divine purpose, nor did you pick out various aspects of your personality. You may think that your desires or specific passions were just randomly acquired. No, my friend! God placed many of those passions inside you. Nobody goes to the superstore of Heaven and says, "I'm going to choose this talent, and I want a little artistic ability, and I want to be a world-class athlete too." No. He put your gifts in you as it pleased *Him*.

You have been specially selected and uniquely equipped. God wants to work through your personality to enable you to fulfill your purpose. God refines us daily to help us get better. We're always working on something—love, patience, wisdom, walking in peace, training our bodies, acquiring new knowledge, not going off on our kids, and so forth. We all can improve in some areas. And that's a good thing. We are all in pursuit of something. But keep in mind that we are deliberately designed.

You have been chosen for this moment in history to use your ability to help manifest God's Kingdom here on the earth. God knew of the wisdom, guidance, and skills that would be needed for our current times. He even knew how to package it so that the people you encounter will receive it. (I'll share more on that in a later chapter.)

Think about this: You could have been born during any time in history, but God waited until now to birth you into the earth. He did so because the world is currently in desperate need of what you carry. The gift, ability, and talent that rests inside of you is not just something; it is *the* thing that humanity needs, your community needs, the marketplace needs, your school needs, and your family needs. We can't do without what you carry, or we will suffer. If you hide what you carry, then you go against God's divine plan. Unknowingly, you hinder His will from being done in your family and in the world. It's time to let God expose the real you to the world.

Society needs the authentic you, because your authenticity carries purpose and power. I like to describe one's purpose as the path of authenticity. The intrinsic qualities that you possess are a result of the specific purpose that was designed for you. But to understand the authentic purpose and path, you have to understand the authentic you.

CARS, PLANES, AND DESTINATIONS

Consider the differences between cars and airplanes. They both can get you from point A to point B, but they don't do it in the same way. A car is designed for ground transportation, and an airplane is designed for air transportation. If you want to get somewhere, like from Chicago to New York for example, you can hop in the car and drive. The different parts of a car help to accomplish the goal of ground transport. The engine, wheels, transmission, axle, carburetor, alternator, throttle, brakes, steering—all these different things help to make up a car. All the components of the car help the car do what it was purposed to do.

Now if you are going from Chicago to London, ground transportation alone cannot get you to your destination. Unless you want to end up on the bottom of the Atlantic Ocean, you need air transportation. Compared to the car, the airplane has a an entirely different set of parts. It has jet engines, wings, rudders, landing gear, and a tail. The jet engines create thrust, which pushes the plane down the runway. Once enough speed has been built up, the plane will begin to lift off into the air due to the wings and design of the plane. All the components of an airplane help it achieve its purpose of air transportation.

No matter how hard you try, you'll never be able to fly the car from one place to another (although modern advancements in technology may change this soon). As it stands currently, a car just doesn't have the necessary parts to make it fly like an airplane. A car's parts and an airplane's parts are specifically designed with their methods of transportation in mind. They are each designed for their specific purpose. For this reason, it is impossible for the car to fulfill the purpose of the airplane, even though they may be headed toward the same destination.

God is the manufacturer, and we are like the airplanes and cars. He has assembled us and put us together with the end in mind. This means that *God has already equipped you with everything you need to get to your destination and achieve your purpose.* Your parts or equipment are the aspects of your unique personality. What's equally important is to know that if you try to go where only the airplane was designed to go, but with automotive parts, you will get frustrated pretty fast. You received all of your parts with the end in mind.

Sometimes we may not like the components of our lives or the things God has put inside us. We may be tempted to complain about our deficient areas and become jealous of other people's natural abilities. But God made you the way you are for a reason. You are hardwired to live out your purpose through your personality and gifts, not *despite* them.

I know this firsthand. Before going into full-time ministry, as I previously mentioned, I was not a good public speaker (or so I thought). I never wanted to be in front or on a stage. I was so much more comfortable with being in the background. Helping to serve without being seen was my comfort zone. So when God called me to speak, I knew I needed His help. I felt ill-equipped to handle this assignment. But I quickly learned that everything I needed was already inside me. I already had the potential to be a great speaker, but I wasn't aware of it yet. Initially, I felt like God was asking

> **"**
> **You are hardwired to live out your purpose through your personality and gifts, not despite them.**
> **"**

me to do something that was not in my DNA. Sometimes we forget that it is God who created us, and He knows what we are capable of better than we do. As I will explain more in a later chapter, sometimes we just need to be exposed to the right conditions or environment for hidden abilities to manifest. Now here I am, many years later, and I am more comfortable speaking to large groups of people than I ever imagined I would be. God knew that what He placed inside of me was enough to get the job done—and done well.

Always remember, *God has put specific things in you that will help you achieve your purpose and destiny.* Because you have those qualities, it is impossible for you to fulfill someone else's purpose and destiny. You might be looking at posts on social media saying, "I want to do that!" But at times, these distractions can become elaborate traps, enticing you to waste your money, time, and energy on something that is not for you. So many people try to become what they see instead of being true to themselves. It's good to be inspired by others. You can glean a lot from others, but you should never try to be who they are instead of embracing who you are.

Pursuing a life outside of what God has planned for you will ultimately leave you feeling frustrated. Some even get mad at God, saying things like, "God, why did you do this to me?" But God will never tell you to pursue a purpose that you were not designed to fulfill. The truth is, you have been equipped to succeed at being you since the day you were born. You have been uniquely designed and pre-qualified to fulfill your purpose. The personality you received is one hundred percent necessary for you to achieve God's purpose. It's critically important for you to understand that you cannot separate the makeup of who you are from your purpose. God needs you to just be *you*. He's counting on it.

FOLLOW THE BREAD CRUMBS

Growing up, I loved to bake. Around my house, I was always baking something, whether it was homemade pizza, cookies, brownies, or bread. I always enjoyed eating fresh-baked foods over store-bought ones. My mom did not buy much junk food at the grocery store. She liked to keep a healthy household, so if I wanted a sweet treat, for the most part I was on my own. However, I was up for the challenge, and homemade brownies became my go-to delicacy of choice. I think my kids inherited my baking gene, because they seem to want to bake chocolate chip cookies every couple weeks. They are terrible for my diet, but they are a blessing to my taste buds.

Due to my affinity for baking, when I was in high school my mom bought a homemade bread maker. I would use that machine all the time. It made the process so easy. Just put in all of the ingredients, set it to the proper setting, and the machine did the rest. In fact, I still have it and use it today. There is nothing like the smell of fresh-baked bread. Cut a few slices, spread some butter on it, and take a seat on the bliss train. Yum!

Often when I make a loaf of bread, I then store it in a sealed bag and place it on our kitchen counter. My kids will often come through the kitchen, see the bread, and quickly cut a slice. I always ask them to use a plate and clean up the crumbs, but that only seems to happen a fraction of the time. I can always tell when one of my younger children has gotten some bread because of the arrangement of the bread crumbs. Those crumbs aren't just around the sealed bag. They start at the kitchen table, trail along the seat, meander across the kitchen floor, and finally end at the counter on the far side of the kitchen where the rest of the loaf is located. I'm sure every parent can relate. (Please clean up your mess, kids.)

I use this example to illustrate the following point. Imagine that the bread crumbs are your unique personality, passions, and proclivities. But the bread itself is your God-given purpose. Without the bread, there can be no bread crumbs. Similarly, the bread crumbs are always indicative that bread is somewhere nearby. In the same way that bread crumbs lead back to the bread, your unique personality leads you back to your purpose.

Here is the secret: *To discover purpose, you have to discover you.* Your authentic self. Most people who are trying to find their purpose are doing it backwards. They are too focused on the *what* instead of the *who*. The *who* is who they really are. Once you discover and commit to who you are created to be, purpose will find you. If you are having trouble finding your purpose in life, don't give up. There is hope! Pursue who you are first. Discover who God has created you to be. Follow the bread crumbs, and you will soon see purpose finding you. Below you will find an exercise that can serve as a starting point for understanding who you are.

EXERCISE: DISCOVERING YOUR PERSONALITY

Get to know yourself better by taking a personality test. This can give you additional insight about how you are designed. It can also serve as an additional tool to help you understand your strengths and weaknesses. After taking the test, review what you have learned. List some of the benefits of having the characteristics that you have. Here is a list of some personality tests that I recommend using:

- **Myers-Briggs Type Indicator**—This is one of the most well-known personality tests, helping individuals understand the different psychological types within behavior. The basic differences are in the way individuals tend to use their perception and make decisions as a result of their interpretation (cost).

- **16 Personalities**—This simple test claims to be "freakishly accurate," helping you learn what really drives, inspires, and worries different personality types, with the goal of helping you build more meaningful relationships. It will help you gain a better understanding of what motivates you. You will also be given helpful comparisons to other well-known influential people, past and present, who have a similar personality type (free).

- *Personality Plus* **by Florence Littauer**— In this book, the author makes a distinction about personalities and temperament, stating "My temperament is the real me; my personality is the dress I put on over me."[2] She then helps readers understand the "real me" by pinpointing strengths and weaknesses in order to improve one's personality. Personalities are then broken up into four major categories. The book maintains a Christian perspective (cost).

- **The Platinum Rule™ (DISC Assessment)**—This test is designed to help you understand your natural behavioral tendencies in everyday situations. Tendencies are broken up into four categories with sixteen sub styles. The term platinum rule comes as an upgrade to the golden rule. Whereas the golden rule says treat others how you would want to be treated, the platinum rule says treat others the way *they* want to be treated. The emphasis here is applying this learned information to improve your existing relationships (cost).

- **John Maxwell Leadership Assessment**—This test is designed to measure your current level of influence, which can then be used to target your leadership growth. You will gain a better understanding of your leadership proficiencies based on Maxwell's Five Levels of Leadership methodology (free and cost versions available).

CHAPTER 4

UNLOCK YOUR IDENTITY

On ministry trips to foreign countries, my dad will often use the morning sessions to teach entrepreneurs and business professionals about leadership. He tells the story of an eagle's egg that accidentally fell out of the nest. The egg rolled down the mountain until it finally found its way into a chicken coop. Soon the egg hatched and the brown eagle came out. But the eagle did not know that he wasn't a chicken. So the brown eagle grew up learning to live like a chicken. He went to chicken school and had chicken friends. He played chicken games and ate like a chicken. But there was one problem—he was an eagle acting like a chicken!

One day, a big eagle spotted him from above and swooped down to ask, "Why are you here in this chicken coop with all of these chickens?"

The brown eagle responded, "What do you mean? I'm a chicken just like them."

The big eagle laughed as he explained his true identity to the brown eagle. After some debate, the big eagle convinced the brown eagle that he could fly. It was hard for the brown eagle to believe since he had not seen any of his chicken friends or family do it before, but he decided to give it a try. He backed up, gave himself some space, and got a running start before taking off. BAM! Instead of flying high, he hit the fence face first.

"I told you I couldn't fly! I told you that I'm not an eagle. I'm a chicken!" he exclaimed.

He demanded that the big eagle leave him and his chicken family alone. The big eagle tried to convince him to try again, but to no avail. So, the big eagle had no choice but to oblige and leave. The brown eagle continued to live, and eventually died, in that same chicken coop with his chicken family. The chicken-eagle fable shows us this one truth: You will live life according to your perceived identity. Misunderstanding your true identity can keep you separated from the life God wants you to live. It can keep you locked into mediocrity and locked out of destiny. Instead of flying high, where you are supposed to be, it will have you living the low life.

> **Misunderstanding your true identity can keep you separated from the life God wants you to live.**

Maybe a few people around you see the potential in you. They encourage you to escape the confines of comfortability, but stepping out feels almost impossible. The good news is, everything is about to change. The things that you once thought were impossible are now possible with God's help. Graduating from college, having a strong marriage, starting a new business or organization, living a prosperous life, getting that big promotion, living your lifelong dream—all of it is possible. The Bible says that with God all things are possible (see Matt. 19:26). Identity is always based on what we choose to identify with. What makes the difference is how we choose to identify ourselves.

WHAT WILL YOUR IDENTITY ALLOW?

In the book of Genesis, we read the story of a man named Abram (later called Abraham). Abram was married to a woman named Sarai. When the story starts, God promises Abram that He will make him a great nation, or people group (see Gen. 12:1–4). Abram was seventy-five years old at the time, and the scripture tells us that Sarai was unable to have children (see Gen. 11:30). But God was not discouraged by their ages or physical condition. Eight years later, the dialogue between God and Abram picks up again. Even though Abram is still childless, God tells Abram that he will have as many descendants as there are stars in the sky (see Gen. 15:1–7).

Since Abram and Sarai couldn't figure out how it was going to happen, they took matters into their own hands. They decided together that Abram would sleep with Sarai's servant, Hagar, and the child born would be their son. So Hagar became pregnant and gave birth to Ishmael. But God still insisted that Sarai would bear them a son. Fast-forward sixteen more years, and both ninety-nine-year-old Abram and ninety-year-old Sarai are well beyond their child-bearing years. But this doesn't faze God one bit. He is finally ready to deliver the promised son to this couple who has waited twenty-four years. I am telling you this whole story because of what happened next.

Before Abram and Sarai could have the child God promised, some things had to change. For many years, they had seen themselves as a couple who could never have children. The barren mindset affected how they viewed God's promise. God then changed their names to change how they saw themselves. One day God said to Abram, "No longer shall your name be called Abram, but your name shall be Abraham; for I have made you a father of many nations" (Gen. 17:5). Abram's name change not only signified a shift in his identity, but also what he was to identify with. For further clarity, let's look at what the two names mean. *Abram* means "exalted father," which is fitting because he had one son, Ishmael.[1] But *Abraham* means "father of a multitude." From now on, his family, servants, and all legal documents referred to him as the *father of a multitude*. When his name changed, so did his identity. Abraham began to mentally reclassify himself. I believe that changing his identity eventually altered his physical body, reversing the effects of time, making it possible for him to have another son and make good on the Lord's promise.

What about Sarai? She was ninety years old and barren. God knew she needed a name change too. God said to Abraham, "...you shall not call her name Sarai, but Sarah shall be her name. And I will bless her and also give you a son by her...and she shall be the mother of nations..." (Gen. 17:15–16). This divine name change eventually led to her bodily functions being supernaturally restored, and she received strength to conceive (see Heb. 11:11). The couple soon conceived and had their promised son, Isaac, a year later. Even though they'd been told they would have a child long before, they couldn't conceive their promised child until their identities were in alignment with the promise.

The story of Abraham and Sarah highlights the importance of how we see ourselves, especially while patiently trusting in God. Here is the point: God could only do in them what their identity would allow. *God can only do in your life what your identity will allow.* If you think you are a loser, it will be hard to find victory even when God has already promised it to you. If you think God has somehow mismanaged your uniqueness or "dealt you a bad hand," you will fail to see the value in how you are made, regardless of the situation. But if you think you are a champion, then you will see God putting you into position to win every time. If you think you are significant, you will find opportunities that affirm your significance.

Your behavior is usually an indicator of what you believe on the inside. Believe God! If your self-image is wrong, then allow God to recalibrate it. Ask Him to help you to see yourself the way He sees you. He will do it because you are His child and He loves you. God is completely committed to your success, but that success starts with your decision.

THE ORIGINAL YOU: MADE IN GOD'S IMAGE

> *Then God said, "Let Us make man in Our image, according to Our likeness; let them have dominion over the fish of the sea, over the birds of the air, and over the cattle, over all the earth and over every creeping thing that creeps on the earth"* (Genesis 1:26).

In this digital age, when we want a program, smartphone app, or piece of software to do something specific, we program it to work that way. Many codes, alphanumeric scripts, and command prompts are combined to execute specific tasks or functions. Nothing digital functions without someone somewhere programming it to function that way. Now think of Adam as an app and God as the great programmer. God used divine code to design our DNA. He got the source code from Himself. Humanity was originally designed (or programmed) to function according to God's image and likeness. His code is flawless. If the software starts malfunctioning, however, it's usually because something or someone has corrupted the programming.

We were originally born and designed in God's image. If we are made in God's image and His likeness, then the more we get to know God, the more we get to know our true selves. Just as Jesus functioned like God, we are to be just like Jesus. The more we get to know God, the more we get in God's presence, the more we understand His ways, and the more we talk with God, the better we will understand how He operates. This leads us to better understand how we were made to operate, because we were made like God.

For example, the Bible says God is love, so when you operate in love, you are functioning the way the Creator made you (see 1 John 4:8). When you're functioning in bitterness and unforgiveness, you literally start malfunctioning from the inside out. Even our physical bodies start to break down when we harbor resentment in our hearts. (Science has proven this mind-body connection to be true on many fronts.) Have you ever been so angry or anxious about something that you couldn't eat even though you should be hungry? This happens because the connection between your mind and your body is strong. But as we operate in God's love, an unconditional love that we are supposed to both receive and convey to others, we find ourselves mentally, emotionally, and physically healthier.

The Bible says, "In the beginning was the Word, and the Word was with God, and the Word was God" (John 1:1). It's vitally important to read the Bible because it is our owner's manual. The Bible tells you everything you need to know about yourself. It tells you who you are, what you have, and what you can do. If you leave it on the shelf and never read it, then you remain in darkness, not knowing your true power or true identity. It teaches us how to win and overcome in every situation, how to maintain a right perspective, and so much more. The more you read God's Word, the more you will find out about your true identity. The more you find your true identity, the more you will discover what you are here to do on this earth. *The Bible is your starting point for purpose, because it's your road map to identity.* The Scripture says, "The entrance of Your words gives light; it gives understanding to the simple" (Ps. 119:130). God gave us His Word to help us rediscover limitless living.

God made us to operate a certain way for optimum efficiency and maximum effectiveness. When we get to know God, we get to know His ways and, correspondingly, His will. This will lead us to discover things about ourselves that we may not have known existed, and that's where the fun begins.

CALIBRATED DESTINY

As I was thinking and writing about identity, I caught a sudden revelation from glancing at my iPhone. The fingerprint scanner on my phone is calibrated to recognize me by a swipe of my finger. (Of course, phones also have facial recognition software.) If I take my friend's phone and try to unlock it with my fingerprint, it displays the message, "Try again." I try again, but to no avail. No matter how many attempts I make to get access, my friend's phone only says, "Try again." It will only accept my friend's fingerprint because it's calibrated to recognize him alone. It will stay locked until his fingerprint is submitted. His fingerprint gives him access to the contents of his phone just as my fingerprint allows me access to my phone's contents. I think we can learn something about our identity from this technology.

Look at your hand. Your fingerprints distinguish you from everyone else. Your destiny is similar in that it's uniquely suited to your own ID. You cannot access somebody else's purpose or destiny with your fingerprint, and nobody else can access your purpose or destiny with their fingerprint. You can't unlock a purpose that's been calibrated to somebody else's identity. Only the authentic you can be granted access to your destiny. *There is no way to counterfeit purpose and destiny.*

It's critically important for you to be your authentic self. Otherwise, you risk your destiny failing to recognize you and telling you, "Try again." This just results in frustration, closed doors, and rejection. If you have suffered any of those things, here's my advice: Be true to yourself. That's the only way you will be able to unlock the destiny that awaits you. Don't try to be someone you are not. Only the real you can go to the place where your authentic expression is required. When God opens a door for you, He's counting on the real you—the authentic you—showing up. You are right for the job. *The authentic you is who you are when you don't have to pretend or put on an act, hide behind a mask, or filter everything you do.* It's the way you think, operate, and see the world without pretense. Being true to yourself is essential to discovering your real purpose in life.

Sometimes, when I was a teenager, I would try to impress some of my peers by acting like someone else. But then when I was around my mom, I would do all of the corny, funny, weird stuff that I would never do in front of my cool friends. That was the real, authentic me. Maybe the authentic you can be kind of awkward, foolish, individualistic, unique, and embarrassing in front of others at times. But it's who you really are. The more you try to hide who you really are, the more you will find that purpose and destiny will hide from you. The moment you accept who God designed you to be is the moment your purpose will begin to unfold.

Be genuine about who you are. My wife was initially attracted to me when she saw my genuineness and honesty. She likes the real me. Being authentic is how I attracted the love of my life and a huge part of my destiny. When you are authentic, you will attract the

> **When you are true to yourself, you will discover more of God's purpose for your life.**

people who are truly supposed to be divinely connected to your life. The more you try to fit into someone else's mold, the more uncomfortable you will become when their personality and purpose don't fit you. When you are true to yourself, you will discover more of God's purpose for your life.

DON'T ABANDON YOURSELF

If you've ever worked with teenagers, been a parent to one, or are currently a teen yourself, you may have noticed that many teens are constantly in search of their identity. Many companies and unbiblical cultural agendas inundate teens with ads and messaging seeking to capitalize on this quest for their *real selves*. Much of this is a demonic manipulation meant to steal the identities of young people rather than inform them.

With that said, we can learn from some more light-hearted examples in the media. You've probably seen at least one movie that portrays the awkward, uncool teen-age guy or girl who goes through a huge transformation and becomes one of the cool kids, only to lose sight of him or herself, and find their world imploding (cue the 1999 classic teen movie *She's All That*). By the time the movie reaches the last act, the main character usually starts to genuinely value his or her true identity and learns a major lesson about being authentic. It's all about a search for identity. That's why it's so common to see teenagers swap friends, change wardrobes, and go through phases year after year. They are on a journey to discover who they are.

When I was a child my mom would take me shop-ping at Sears. She would make me try on all kinds of clothing. It seemed like I tried on a dozen jeans, shoes, and shirts that didn't fit right. It was like torture. To this day my wife, Niki, laughs at my consistent refusal to try on anything at a clothing store. It takes an act of God to get me to try on some jeans. Because of this, sometimes I end up with something that doesn't fit right. Then I have to go through the hassle of taking it back to the store either for an exchange or refund. (I know what you might be thinking and yes, it would just be easier to try them on the first time.)

These days, many of us prefer online shopping, but the downside is that most times you can't try something on until you've bought it. Imagine buying a pair of shoes that looked stylish online, but when you put them on, they pinched and rubbed your feet in all the wrong places.

Similarly, sometimes in life we decide to identify with things that don't really fit us. It's up to us to realize that they don't fit and make the necessary adjustments. When you try to wear something that's too small or too big, it won't look right or feel comfortable on you. The same thing happens when we try to assume an identity that doesn't fit how we've been designed by God. Your personality was custom designed for you, and God knew exactly what would complement your destiny.

> **Your personality was custom designed for you, and God knew exactly what would complement your destiny.**

You might be trying to be like a friend you admire, a musician, a powerful minister, a business mogul, or some popular YouTuber. The truth is that the world has enough Beyoncés, and she's the only one of her kind. When you focus too much on the gifts and talents of others, you can unknowingly start to question and abandon your own. Whenever you envy someone else's ability, you automatically devalue yours. I like what Craig Groeschel, senior pastor of Life Church says, "The quickest way to kill something special is to compare it with something else."[2]

Stop comparing! You are special—so act like it. Don't give up on yourself. Stop thinking about how much you want to be like someone else. You can't fulfill your purpose pretending to be someone else. Don't give up on your purpose, your dream, and the person God has called you to be. The world needs you exactly the way you were designed. The best is yet to come.

FIXING A BROKEN IDENTITY

You were created in the image of God, so the shape of your identity starts with Him. Any identity crisis ends when we connect with the one who gave the identity. We need to go back to the manufacturer.

The first step to changing your negative self-image is to agree with God. Learn to be okay with just being you. Accept that God didn't make you faulty. You are going to be you for a long time. But if you are constantly trying to escape yourself, life will no longer be an adventure, but rather a prison. Don't hold the real you hostage. Instead of trying to get away from yourself, learn to enjoy yourself. Remember, God sees you as strong, courageous, brilliant, creative, and special.

Abram/Abraham changed his situation through his words. He spoke something different, and as a result, he began to see a different reality. According to the *illusory truth effect*, psychologists say that if you want to convince yourself that something is true, regardless of it being true or not, you just have to do one simple thing. Repeat it—over and over and over again.[3] Over time, because of how our brains are designed, your mind will start to receive it as truth, first subconsciously, then consciously. This means that you must declare who you are and who you want to be before you see it as a reality. The change you are looking for lies in what you say about yourself.

I have actually done this exercise myself and seen great results. Several years ago, the Lord prompted me to write something on a Post-It note and stick it to the inside of my Bible. Here's what I wrote:

> I am a gifted author, speaker, and communicator of the gospel and of wisdom. Thank You, Lord, for using me to lead revival in my nation and in this generation. I am a world-renowned leader and a next-generation general of faith.

As a result of writing this and saying it every day, I have developed an online leadership course called the Winston Leadership Institute, where hundreds of people have been trained to be better leaders. I was approached by a publisher to publish my first book, *Strong in Spirit: 5 Minute Devotions for Preteen Boys,* which I co-wrote with my wife Niki. Opportunities, engagements, and situations seeking my wisdom became commonplace. I could go on, but you get the point. And God gets all of the credit, because without His direction and prompting, none of it would have happened.

Here's what you must know: None of those situations just happened. The words I spoke shifted my identity because they declared something new for me to identify with. Here's my second point: If I had not rewritten my "software" by saying those things consistently, I would have passed up those opportunities, because I would have felt like they didn't fit me—like they weren't *for* me. I could have felt like they were for someone smarter, more well educated, more creative, who has more experience.

We all want opportunities in life but it is possible to unknowingly let the opportunities God has custom designed for us slip right past us because we thought they were for someone else. Through a subconscious devaluing of your own identity, it is possible that you have missed out on some of the things that others now have. Maybe you found yourself being envious of someone recently, but really you're just mad that they had the courage and self-worth necessary to say *yes*. You don't need to be jealous. Jealousy is just fear that you don't have as much value as someone else. But that's a lie. Jealousy is unnecessary when you know who you are and the value you hold. Repair your identity by doing the exercise below.

EXERCISE: RIGHT PERSON FOR THE ASSIGNMENT

On an index card, write down three things that you want to accomplish over the next year. On the other side of the card, write down who you have to be or what you have to do well to accomplish those goals. For example, on one side you can write, "I want to write a book." On the other side you can write, "I am a talented writer and author." Take what you have written and say it out loud every day.

CHAPTER 5

EMBRACE BEING THE UNDERDOG

Defeat is something we all face at some time in our lives. It could be in a sporting match, in the loss of a contract you hoped to win for your business, in a rejection from a college you hoped to attend, or many other scenarios. Defeat can be tough. No one likes to feel like they are losing. Even more so, no one likes to feel like winning is not possible.

I remember the feeling when an ex-girlfriend told me the relationship was over. I remember how my heart dropped when I got laid off of a new job that I had taken just two months into my marriage. I remember the feelings of panic, disappointment, and despair. I will never forget the hopelessness I felt when I bombed my ACT exam in my junior year of high school. That poor performance left me feeling so bad that I began to think maybe life was not worth living. Maybe I'm not the person for the dream that I have. Maybe things are better without me. At times in life, many of us have felt like the underdog or that winning was just not possible.

Life is a journey that requires patience, strength, trust in God, and a commitment to development. You have to trust that God will help you become everything you need to be to fulfill your destiny. You cannot achieve what the Creator has purposed for you to achieve without becoming who He has called you to be. At times, you might feel like David the shepherd boy from the Bible. Everything in his life seemed to indicate he was overlooked and undervalued. But that was not the truth. When the prophet Samuel came to anoint the next king of Israel, God told him: "Do not look at his appearance or at his physical stature..." (1 Sam. 16:7).

When He said this, God was not talking to Samuel about David, but about Eliab, David's oldest brother. When Samuel came to the house of Jesse to anoint the new king, he asked Jesse to bring all his sons to him. Jesse brought them all, except David, who he thought was the least likely to be chosen. Even Samuel judged Eliab by his appearance. He was tall, handsome, and strong. He probably looked like he hit the gym several times a week. Samuel could have assumed God would probably choose him.

But the Lord said to Samuel, "Do not consider his appearance or his height, for I have rejected him. The Lord does not look at the things people look at. People look at the outward appearance, but the Lord looks at the heart" (1 Samuel 16:7 NIV).

Then the Lord chose David. David was such an unlikely candidate that his father hadn't even bothered to call him in when parading the rest of his brothers in front of Samuel. Imagine how you would feel if this happened to you. You might feel like your family didn't think much of you. But it doesn't matter what other people think. It only matters what God says. It doesn't matter if other people discount you or don't think you look the part. It doesn't matter where you come from either. What matters is that God can use you if you let Him! All that mattered was that David's heart was right for the assignment.

The Bible says God chose you because you are special to Him:

> [God] *has saved us and called us with a holy calling, not according to our works, but according to His own purpose and grace which was given to us in Christ Jesus before time began* (2 Timothy 1:9).

God's purpose for you is true. His Word about you is true. And His calling for you is true, regardless of what you think it looks like. God wants to use you, and

He's pursuing you. You are not here by some random chance. God chose you to be here on the earth at this very moment, for a reason.

GOD HAS EQUIPPED YOU

After David was anointed king, he faced a giant-sized problem. The problem's name was Goliath, and he was the captain of the Philistine army. Some theologians estimate he was almost ten feet tall.[1] He verbally taunted the Israelite army every day for many days. Every day the Israelite army showed up to the battlefield in the valley of Elah, but nobody fought. The Israelites were afraid of Goliath, but David soon grew tired of the Philistine's threats and decided to step up and fight him. Nobody asked David to do it. He volunteered for the job. He seized the opportunity to serve his people.

Many people have heard the story of David and Goliath, in which David, the perceived underdog, beats all the odds and defeats Goliath and the Philistine army. But what I want to point out to you is what happened right after David decided to fight and right before he entered into battle. This is the conversation that King Saul had with David:

> *...And Saul said to David, "Go, and the Lord be with you!" So Saul clothed David with his armor, and he put a bronze helmet on his head; he also clothed him with a coat of mail. David*

fastened his sword to his armor and tried to walk, for he had not tested them. And David said to Saul, "I cannot walk with these, for I have not tested them." So David took them off. Then he took his staff in his hand; and he chose for himself five smooth stones from the brook, and put them in a shepherd's bag, in a pouch which he had, and his sling was in his hand. And he drew near to the Philistine (1 Samuel 17:37–40).

David was about to fight Goliath, so Saul tried to give him some armor. It makes sense. Who would willingly fight a ten-foot giant without any armor? David took the armor, but then realized that he couldn't walk in it. Saul was "taller than any of the people from his shoulders upward" (1 Sam. 10:23). Saul was very tall, like a professional basketball player. His armor was custom fit to his measurements, and it was probably heavy too. Saul tried to give David something that worked for him (Saul), but it was not a fit for David. It was too big and too heavy. David eventually went back to what he knew would work for him: a few stones and a sling.

Sometimes other people will try to give us the things they think we need, maybe even things that worked for them. Just like Saul tried to give David his armor, people will try to equip us for our journey the way they were equipped. But what worked for Saul was not what God wanted David to use. As a matter of fact, David probably would have died trying to use Saul's armor. If David had listened to Saul's suggestion, he could have been defeated in battle. He couldn't use the weapons or the strategy that made sense for someone else. He must have said to himself, "This isn't me! This is not who I am, and this is not how I'm going to do battle." Even when it doesn't make sense to other people, following your God-given instincts will not steer you wrong. Follow God, and you will always find success.

So David went back to what he knew: stones and a sling. It was commonplace during those times for shepherds to use a sling and stone to ward off beasts that would try to attack the sheep, such as lions or bears. A sling and a stone in the hands of an experienced slinger was a very dangerous weapon. David had a weapon he was very confident in, but it was a weapon Saul was not confident in. David had to have confidence in the way God was directing him to use his sling and stones. The application of his unique skill took courage. Courage that no one else seemed to have. And this led young David to victory over Goliath.

> **Staying true to your identity will lead to victory and pave the way to your destiny.**

Here's my point: Staying true to your identity will lead to victory and pave the way to your destiny. Your identity is who you are at your core. To get the victory, you have to be true to who God has designed you to be. I have had many people give me suggestions and opinions on what they thought I should do or how they thought I should handle a situation. Some of those recommendations were good, some were bad, and some were just time wasters. One thing is for certain: If I don't get instructions from God and stay true to who God has created me to be, then I will end up frustrated.

God knows what you need and how you function best. Imagine how frustrated David would have been trying to fight with Saul's armor. He literally would have aborted victory. Stay true to yourself and listen to God, and you will find yourself on the way to the top.

CORRECTING YOUR UNDERSTANDING

David naturally seemed to gravitate to the battle with Goliath. No one coerced him to go. He was delivering food to his brothers at the battlefield, and he saw something wrong. He wasn't even old enough to fight in the Israelite army. Yet God put the desire in David's heart to defend his people.

Something we can learn from the story of David is that we all have innate passions that God has deposited in our hearts. We didn't create them. They exist through divine providence. We then have to get the right interpretation of those passions, because our passions can lead us to our purpose. It then takes the Holy Spirit to help us correctly frame our purpose and passions.

For example, when I was six years old I wanted to be a cardiologist. I would walk around telling people that I wanted to be a heart surgeon when I grew up. But when people asked me why I wanted to be a cardiologist, I couldn't tell them. I wasn't trying to be coy or difficult. I genuinely did not know. It was an innate passion deep inside of me. I wasn't mature enough to fully analyze it, but I was old enough to recognize the feeling of it. For years that was my story. I never even considered anything else as a career. I just knew that I was born to be a cardiologist.

It wasn't until my last year of college that the Lord spoke to me and showed me something that I would never forget. He said, "David, I have called you to do heart surgery, but not in the way that you think. You have assumed that you would operate on the natural hearts of people, but I have called you to do spiritual heart surgery. You will help to heal broken hearts in the spirit. You have been called by Me to be a spiritual cardiologist."

I was amazed at what God was speaking to me at that moment. I had misunderstood the calling of God for my life. I didn't *miss* it, but I did misunderstand it. I learned that the correct understanding of the gift that I have is just as important as the gift itself.

Can you identify a deep passion within you that you've had since you were young? Maybe it's something you could never get away from or turn off, no matter how hard you tried. Maybe it's something that needs divine insight applied to it. Let God show you how He sees you and your future. If we do not have the correct perspective, we will only go by what we know. We will default to the most common version of our situation. We will see other people who look like us, who have similar backgrounds, and see how they are exe-

> **Every path will look different because your personality determines your path.**

cuting their dreams. Human nature is to mimic what we see in hopes of getting the same results. But only God can show you your authentic path. Every path will look different because your personality determines your path.

God made you to see and perceive with your natural and spiritual eyes. With your natural eyes you are only seeing a fragment of reality, but you can see much more of what God wants to show you with your spiritual perception. Sometimes the picture God paints won't make sense to you at first. But that's okay, because it's designed to grow your faith. Like my dad always says, "God's ways aren't designed to make sense; they are designed to make faith." All you have to do is believe. Many people get tripped up, because they think that what they see with their natural perception is the full extent of their gift. But the reality is, you can do so much more.

WINNING IN THE WAITING ROOM

"When is the package going to arrive?" "How long will this download take?" "How long will it take to get through this traffic?" "When will we get the results back?" We spend a lot of our lives playing the waiting game. We go to the store and have to wait in line to check out. We drive to work and have to wait ten minutes for the train to pass before we can continue our commute. We call customer service about our purchase and wait on hold for the next available representative. We teach our kids the virtue of patience. We all have to wait.

The waiting room at the hospital can be one of the most challenging, frustrating, and stressful places to exercise patience—especially when you're in the emergency room. When you arrive, the receptionist tells you to have a seat and promises that they will call you when they are ready for you. Sometimes you have no idea how long you'll have to wait to be seen. That's the most stressful part.

Every person pursuing purpose has to endure the waiting room. Every gift has to be able to withstand a dry season, a season of waiting and feeling forgotten. The waiting room can be tough, because it can make you second guess yourself and over-analyze what you may have done wrong to get stuck there. But the fact is, doing everything right is what may have brought you into the waiting room.

We see this principle at work in the life of Jesus. Jesus was about thirty years old when He began His ministry (see Luke 3:23). Jesus didn't start right out of high school or college. He had to *wait*. The Son of God had to endure the waiting room just like we do. He had to wait until God's divine timing released Him.

In the Bible, Joseph went to prison before he ascended to power over Egypt. He was falsely accused of a crime he didn't commit and ended up in prison for two years (see Gen. 41:1). The prison was Joseph's waiting room. He appealed to a fellow inmate to put in a good word for him when he was released, but that man forgot about Joseph as soon as he made it out. (I will share more about Joseph in later chapters.)

Many of us can relate to feeling forgotten. The job referral, the new contract, the business opportunity, the speaking invitation or music gig, the special favor to help get you a promotion, the promise of resources, the help you were pledged—all forgotten. No matter who has disappointed you, know that God has not forgotten you. He has kept detailed and accurate records of everything that has happened in your life. Take comfort in knowing that God can never mismanage your life. Don't lose hope. Don't drop your faith. Don't get mad at people. The Bible reminds us that promotion does not come from people, but ultimately it comes from the Lord (see Ps. 75:6–7). People are not in control of your promotion. God is your promoter.

MY WAITING ROOM

I know something about the waiting room from personal experience. In 2009, when I first started in full-time ministry, I was excited and zealous to start my new journey. I didn't know much of what I was doing, but I was ready to put everything I had into it. People soon found out that I was in ministry like my dad, and they started inviting me to speak at their churches and events. I thought these were great opportunities, but God had me pump the brakes.

One morning as I was praying, I heard God say loud and clear, "Build My house, not your kingdom." I knew what that meant. God was telling me that it was not time for that part of my purpose to be executed. He told me to wait. So for the next seven years I didn't accept any traveling speaking engagements. I declined almost every invitation I received in obedience to the Holy Spirit. I would graciously respond telling them that the Lord had not released me to go into that season of ministry yet. He wanted me to focus on building the local church and youth ministry. So that's what I did, and as a result, I entered the waiting room.

In that season, I continued to do ministry. The Greek word translated as *ministry* means "service."[2] I wasn't sitting around doing nothing while I waited. I served. The scripture encourages us to wait on the Lord and be of good courage (see Ps. 27:14). This word *wait* reminds me of the term we use for servers at a restaurant, *waiters*. When you eat at a restaurant, you usually don't see the waiters wandering around aimlessly (or at least you shouldn't). If they are good waiters, they will serve their customers by taking their orders and bringing food and drinks to their tables promptly. Then they will check on the customers regularly to make sure they are pleased with what was served. One of the keys to winning in the waiting room is to continue to serve God and others around you in excellence. Learn to be faithful right where you are at. Look for ways that you can be a blessing and help someone else on their journey of purpose. Don't stop serving. *Serving always makes you a candidate for promotion.* And when you are faithful in the little, as a byproduct you will develop the habits necessary to take care of something bigger.

While I was waiting and serving, I still had to trust that God knew best. I had confidence that those opportunities, especially the notable ones, would come back around when it was time. And now I can say that the invitations have come back in multiplied fashion. My part was to wait on God's timing.

FAITH AND PATIENCE

Sometimes, when we have to wait for a long time, we can start to boil over with frustration. We feel this way because we can't logically understand why it should be taking this long. When you're waiting with God you will have some seasons when you know why you are waiting and some seasons when you don't. Don't allow yourself to get frustrated. Don't try to leave the waiting room prematurely and bust down the door of destiny. Wait until God calls you to move. You will know because He will open the door for you, just like a good gentleman. One of my favorite scriptures is found is the book of Proverbs: "Trust in the Lord with all your heart, and lean not on your own understanding; in all your ways acknowledge Him, and He shall direct your paths"(Prov. 3:5–6).

The waiting room is a place of faith. Faith is continuing to walk with God even when you can't see where the path is headed. Faith doesn't require full understanding. It just requires full obedience. Faith breeds confidence, but trust breeds commitment. While you are waiting, exercise patience. Patience is being consistently consistent with your believing. We have to expect the best from God and then be fully committed to His way of doing things. That's what it means to trust in the Lord.

Your promotion in life has a lot to do with how you respond to your waiting room. You may see others all around you in their season of elevation, and this could tempt you to follow their lead. Comparing your waiting room season to the current season of others can tempt you to disobey God or *leave* the waiting room early. This is a trap. Remember what I said earlier: You can't fulfill your purpose pretending to be someone else. I like what DeVon Franklin says:

> It's our differences, our uniqueness, that gets us to where we are supposed to be in life—our God-given destiny. It's not about trying to transform yourself into a vision of who other people want you to be or who your employer wants you to be. Understand what's required for your job but do it in a way that is authentically you.[3]

Instead of imitating what another person is doing, keep doing what you've been doing as your authentic self. If something needs to change while you wait, God will make it clear to you. Just listen and obey.

The late Kobe Bryant, legendary Los Angeles Lakers basketball player, once said, "I don't want to be the next Michael Jordan. I only want to be Kobe Bryant." That attitude pushed him to be the best he could be, and his hard work paid off. Kobe ended his career in 2016 with 33,643 total points, which put him third on the all-time scoring list—just ahead of Michael Jordan.[4]

If you want to continue to rise, then you have to forget about the plateau. Forget about feeling that you will only get so far in life—that you've hit the ceiling. Keep serving God and hold on to your declaration of faith. Remain committed to God's timeline, and you will find your way to the top. The more faithful you are, the better you position yourself to allow your greatness to emerge.

> **If you want to continue to rise, then you have to forget about the plateau.**

EXERCISE: YOUR FUTURE IS NOW

For thirty days, make a decision to step into the future. Modify your daily routine to include an activity that aligns with your future. Being disciplined in the waiting room will always benefit you in any season of your life. Choose from one of the suggestions below or come up with something unique for you.

- Read a leadership book. (*The Leadership Challenge: How to Make Extraordinary Things Happen in Organizations,* by Kouzes and Posner, is a good one.)
- Exercise for thirty minutes a day, four days per week.
- Make a healthy dietary change (i.e. only eat sweets one day per week or eliminate soda).

- Adjust your spending habits to save an additional 5–10 percent of your income.
- Eliminate a specific bad habit.
- Be ten minutes early to everything.
- Or create your own challenge.

CHAPTER 6

POTENTIAL: YOUR DOORWAY TO GREATNESS

In 2003, a young, talented basketball player was drafted to the NBA straight out of high school. After some years in the league, he decided that he wanted to go to the next level in how he played the game, specifically in the area of three-point shots. He wanted to win a championship, and he knew he had to get better in order to lead his team to victory. He hired a sports psychologist to help him achieve his goal. The specialist worked to train the player's mind using a method called visualization. He wanted the player to see himself successfully making three-point shots.

The specialist recommended creating an eight to twelve-minute highlight video of the player successfully making various three-point shots: spot-up shots, off the dribble shots, and more. The specialist even recommended adding some of the player's favorite songs to the video to help him associate his actions with positive feelings. The player was required to watch it every night before bed to stimulate his subconscious to replay the images while he slept. Finally, the sports psychologist instructed him to make a minimum of four hundred three-point shots every day while imagining the best defender guarding him. He did this for the next few years. As a result, the player went from shooting 33 percent to making over 40 percent of his attempted three-point shots by the 2012–13 season, which is very good. You may be familiar with this player. His name is LeBron James. His team at the time, the Miami Heat, also won the NBA championship that same year.[1]

How you see yourself will dictate how far you can go in life. LeBron wanted to go farther, so he had to see himself going farther. He had to meditate on the reality that he was trying to create. Here is the principle that I want you never to forget: *Your thinking will always seek to take you to the place where it can express itself the most.* Some call it a mindset. Others refer to it as a belief system. However you choose to refer to it, it's extremely important. It will either empower or suppress your success. You may have great potential, but that potential will always be limited by your mentality.

PART 1: DISCOVERING YOUR POTENTIAL

In science, we learn about something called potential energy, which is the energy an object has because of its position, rather than its motion. Potential energy describes what could be, but has yet to be expressed. The potential inside of you, placed there by God, represents what could, be but has yet to be expressed. Potential is everything you could be in life, in seed form. It is your hidden ability, your concealed greatness. Others may not know about your ability. You might not know about all of your abilities, but the ability is there, nonetheless.

God placed your potential inside you—within your spirit—before you were even born. In fact, your potential is defined by God. Remember, your full capacity is big, because you were created in God's image.

The Bible paints a picture of our full potential and authority, "God stands in the congregation of the mighty; He judges among the gods…. I said, 'You are gods, and all of you are children of the Most High'" (Ps. 82:1,6). In the New Testament, Jesus pointed out that in the law of Moses, God said, "You are gods" (John 10:34). In other words, you were made like God. The Hebrew word for *god* in this scripture is *elohim*, which is translated as "mighty men."[2] The extent and the limit of our potential is to be like God. We are not God, but we are to imitate Him. Everything that Jesus did as the Son of God, we can do. Jesus said that if you believe in Him, you can do greater things than He did (see John 14:12). This revelation is necessary for you to realize your potential. The potential is in you to do great things.

I may not know you personally, but I know my God, and I know He has put great potential within everyone whom He has created.

ACCESSING YOUR POTENTIAL

The question we must all consider is how do we manifest our potential for greatness? The potential God has placed inside of us usually has to be squeezed out. In fact, potential works a lot like toothpaste. If I open a tube and turn it upside down, nothing happens. Turning the toothpaste upside down doesn't get the toothpaste onto my toothbrush. Because it is a paste, I have to squeeze the tube to get the contents out. Your potential works the same way; it responds to the demand being placed upon it. Some form of pressure needs to be applied. Potential has to be pushed out for you to reap the benefits.

I remember feeling this way when I first started leading in my church. I was in my early twenties and had just started overseeing both the church's youth ministry and all operations for Bill Winston Ministries, a global outreach ministry organization. I felt underqualified and unprepared. I didn't know if I could do what was being asked of me. I was overwhelmed and desperately asking God for His help. But the pressure I felt unlocked wisdom, creativity, leadership capacity, and speaking abilities I never knew I had. God showed me that everything necessary for my assignment was already inside of me. I just needed to listen and trust Him to bring it to the surface. I needed to allow the pressure to do its work. The same is true for you. Whatever you need for your assignment is already hidden inside of you.

As you let God direct your steps on your journey, He will often lead you to things for which you feel inadequately prepared. Situations or circumstances may require something from you that you feel you don't possess. You may have it, but you just can't see it. But God can see it. He put it there. That's potential. As I said before, potential is simply hidden ability. I've heard potential referred to as unused success. You just have to let God put you in the position where your potential can come out and success can be realized.

In his book, *Revelation of Royalty*, my father writes:

> Some [people] have all the right ingredients inside of them but can't flourish because they are not in the proper soil. As with an acorn, everything you will become is already inside of you—God is not adding anything anymore; he's developing what's already there.[3]

Potential doesn't come out of us without work. Work is important. Work is biblical. God uses work to develop us. After God created the garden of Eden, on the seventh day the Bible says that He rested from all of His work (see Gen. 2:3). When He was creating something new, it was called *work*. It goes on to say that God put humans in the garden to *tend* it (see Gen. 2:15). The Greek word, *abad,* used here for *tend,* means "to work."[4] God put Adam and Eve to work after He placed them in Eden. This was absolutely necessary because it was the only way they could discover their potential. *As potential is released, purpose is revealed.* Jesus says we are to let our light shine so people can see our good *works* and glorify our Father in Heaven (see Matt. 5:16). In the Kingdom of God, work is not an option. It's a mandate because it is how we discover who we really are so we may bring glory to God.

Here are eight reasons why work is important:

1. Work is the way you can give something of value to the world.

2. Work releases and develops your gifts and talents.

3. Work keeps you mentally healthy by focusing your mind on something productive.

4. Work is a means by which dreams, ideas, and goals become a reality.

5. Work makes you a blessing to other people.

6. Work allows you to become a co-creator with God.

7. You will not fulfill your potential and purpose in God's Kingdom without work.

8. Work provides avenues by which revenues can be directed into your hands supernaturally, avenues through which God can give you more seed to sow.[5]

The demand or *pressure* on your potential may come from school, your job, an assignment, a leadership position, a promotion, the birth of a new organization or business, ministry, volunteering, writing a book, getting married, becoming a parent, etc. Until pressure is applied, your potential remains hidden, even from you. You will always know when potential is coming out because the pressure being applied can make you feel uncomfortable and out of your league. But stay with it. It's good for you. It's God's plan working in your life.

PART 2: GROWING INTO YOUR POTENTIAL

If you grew up in an urban area like I did, chances are you probably don't know much about farming. I have never enjoyed gardening or growing plants, so I don't know much about it. I've heard farmers say that you can only plant the same kind of seed in the same soil for so long. After about seven years of planting the same kind of seed, you have to switch to something else, which is called *turning crops*. This is a necessary step because certain plants demand specific minerals from the soil. After so long, the dirt is depleted of those minerals and will no longer successfully grow those same plants. So the farmer has two options: either change the seed or go to a different patch of land. Otherwise, the future growth of those crops will be in jeopardy. The environment determines what the seed produces.

God first created Adam outside of the garden of Eden. Then he *put* him, or we can say *planted* him, inside of the garden, the very place where he was assigned to express his purpose. God commanded Adam and Eve to "be fruitful, multiply, fill the earth, subdue it, and have dominion" over all the other creatures (Gen. 1:28). Then Adam began to name every creature that was presented to him in the garden of Eden. If Adam was not planted in the garden of Eden, it would have been impossible for him to fulfill his purpose. His purpose required that he be planted in the right environment.

> **The purpose and potential that God has placed in you needs the right environment to flourish.**

Your situation is no different. The purpose and potential that God has placed in you needs the right environment to flourish. A seed always needs to be placed in the right environment to grow. A seed cannot grow if it's not planted. A seed needs certain things in order to grow, and the environment supplies what is needed. Likewise, you need a certain set of conditions to grow into who you were created to be.

Every seed has to die in order to ultimately become what it was created to be. God's intent is not for you to die naturally, but rather to let the old version of you expire. This will yield a newer version of your character—allowing you to more readily release your greatness. It's time to let God shift you into the environment you need in order to grow.

GET IN THE ZONE

A few years ago, I attempted to do some landscaping in our yard. I had zero experience and had no clue what I was doing. I watched a few home and garden shows, read a few materials, and gave it a try. It was a failed (and expensive) attempt to say the least, but I learned something valuable. I learned that certain plants are designed for specific geographic zones. The plants won't fully bloom unless they are in the right environment and the right geographical location. I found that out the hard way. It wasn't that I had faulty plants. It was that I was trying to get them to flourish in the wrong environment.

The same is true for us. We are the seeds, and God is the planter. *Your environment is the soil that nurtures the seed of who you are into full development.* Where God places you ultimately serves as a catalyst to your growth. Parts of your personality will not blossom, in full, until you get into the right environment. I have personally seen this happen in my life as well as the lives of many others. My character has matured as the pursuit of my purpose became more intense and I allowed myself to be planted in the right environments.

All the environments that God is placing you into are meant to expose the potential inside of you. You are stronger, more gifted, and better equipped than you think. Your potential is just greatness in the embryonic form. Let it develop. Don't leave the environment because it's hard. Let the environment do its job. Soon you will see your potential bloom into something beautiful.

FINDING THE RIGHT ENVIRONMENT

The right environment for you is the environment that almost seems to be lacking something that your gifts, talents, personality, and abilities can provide. It is the place or situation that is ready to receive what you have to offer. Here are six simple questions to ask yourself to help you identify if an environment is right for you:

1. Does it pull on something that your heart has already been meditating on?

2. Does it present an opportunity that lines up with your goals or purpose?

3. Are people in this environment willing and able to help you develop?

4. Does it intimidate you because you feel like you're not ready for it yet?

5. Can they benefit from your presence?

6. Can God help you grow there?

In the book of Genesis, we read the story of Joseph, the eleventh son of Jacob. God gave him big dreams, but he experienced serious hardship. (We will talk about the story of Joseph in detail in a later chapter.) Just when things seemed darkest, Joseph discovered that he could interpret dreams. He interpreted the dreams of a few of the fellow prisoners, not knowing that this hidden ability would later get him promoted to the palace. When Pharaoh called him from the prison to interpret his dream, Joseph did so with such wisdom and skill that he immediately got promoted to second-in-charge over all of Egypt. The ability that he discovered in the least desirable environment eventually led to his promotion to the most distinguished environment. It was the environment that brought out Joseph's hidden ability or potential. Without the right environment, development is handicapped. Never underestimate the power of being in an environment conducive to growth.

The Bible indicates that we can do all things through Christ who strengthens us (see Phil. 4:13). His strength gives us the power to overcome all things. God's ability is not conditional. You can do everything that God wills for you to do through Christ (the Anointed One and His anointing). Some of the tasks and projects that come your way, which you really don't like, are actually pushing potential out of you. If you sit around doing nothing, your potential has no way to come out of you. Remember, potential must have a demand placed on it. If you run from opportunities that pressure you, your potential will stay locked up inside of you.

Potential is more than just hidden ability. It's untapped power and hidden strength. We all have it. Don't discount the plan of God because you don't think you are capable enough. Greatness is inside of you waiting to be released.

PART 3: THE REFINING PROCESS

As God takes us through the process of exposing our potential, He is simultaneously refining our character. As our character is being refined, our gifts and special abilities are being refined as well. The refining process is like cooking meat. Nobody wants to order a steak, chicken, or other piece of meat at a restaurant and receive an uncooked piece of meat. Now the raw, unseasoned meat and the seasoned cooked meat are still the same piece of meat, but the cooked one is more palatable than the raw one. It has become more desirable due to the cooking or *refining* process. As you continue to be shaped into the image of Christ, your process of refinement is preparing you and your gifts to become more palatable to the world.

The refining process is also necessary for turning raw gold nuggets into beautiful pieces of jewelry. The gold nuggets are purified by fire. After the metal is heated and refined to a certain level, the gold is identified as 10-karat gold. But this is one of the lowest levels of refinement

> **" As you continue to be shaped into the image of Christ, your process of refinement is preparing you and your gifts to become more palatable to the world. "**

because it took the least amount of time in the fire. In order to increase the purity of the gold, the metal needs to be heated for a longer time. Gold can be purified into 14-karat, 18-karat, and even 24-karat gold. The 24-karat gold is considered pure, because it has gone through the most rigorous purification process. It also happens to be the most valuable type of gold. This is because it remained in the fire longer.

The process for purifying gold is a good metaphor for what happens in our own lives. Sometimes it feels like God is allowing us to go through the fires of life. Naturally, we don't like it, and we want out of the fire. We ask God to excuse us from this trial, but God allows us to grow through it. He never promised that life would be easy, but He did promise to give us strength and to be with us through it all. The refining fires of life have a purpose: They are building us, shaping us, and removing the impurities from our hearts. The more we go through the refining fire, the purer we become. As our purity increases, more value is added to our gift.

Maybe you feel like you have the talent, potential, and skills, but nobody seems to want what you have to offer. The answer is to continue to go through the refining process. When you let God work on you, help you, assist you, and make you better, it's like cooking the meat. It makes you more palatable for those who are receiving what you have to offer. They will ask for and salivate after your gift rather than resisting it. We all have God-given skills and abilities, but it's up to you to enroll in the refinement process that will prepare you for presentation to the world.

You may say to yourself, "Why don't they want to listen to my song, read my book, watch my content, or hear my idea?" As good as your content may be, it just may not be time yet for others to be exposed to it. And sometimes the audience that God has earmarked for you will be different than the audience that is in front of you now. At this moment, God might not allow you to be in some rooms or around some people because they have not yet cultivated a taste for what you bring to the table.

You are specific and unique, and you carry exactly what someone needs. *You are someone's future favorite.* So if it seems like people don't prefer what you have to offer right now, don't sweat it! Just focus on being a blessing to those who are in front of you at the moment. Don't be in a hurry. Your audience is

> **You are specific and unique, and you carry exactly what someone needs. You are someone's future favorite.**

being prepared as you are reading this book. The truth is, people receive you so much better when they *value* what you carry.

I believe at times God will obscure our greatness from us to motivate us to be more dependent on Him. He knows that as we truly start to grasp the reality of our own greatness, the temptation to become dependent on ourselves grows. Pride tries to convince us that we can meet all of our own needs, independent of direction from or submission to God. This is why God takes us on the journey—to fortify our humility and solidify our allegiance.

I would never have done many of the things I've accomplished in my life if God hadn't led me into them. To see your potential produce results and your dream become a reality, you need to do some work. Don't be scared off by a little hard work, because it's working to bring you closer to your destiny. It's also simultaneously facilitating the uncovering of your uniqueness.

I challenge you to maximize your potential. The potential of an apple seed is to become an apple tree, not just one apple. If many more seeds are planted, then eventually we'll see an apple orchard. That's called maximizing potential—when the releasing of your potential helps to unlock the potential in others. A single apple seed doesn't look like much, but it has great potential if planted. Without being planted, the potential inside the seed cannot be released. However, discovery is always the first step to a life of fulfillment. Discover your potential. Next, allow it to grow and blossom. Lastly, let God prepare it for mass distribution by refining it. God is pruning you so that you will produce even more fruit (see John 15:2). Someone is looking forward to enjoying your fruit!

EXERCISE: DISCOVERING SOLUTIONS

Think about all of the different issues that your city, town, or metropolitan area is currently facing. If you could solve one problem in your city, what would it be and why? It could be related to crime, violence, poverty, education, socioeconomic issues, faith-based organizations, housing, special interest groups, or specific ethnic groups. These are a handful of examples, but it could be something else entirely. Considering this may give you insight into what things are important to you and where your gifts could flourish the most.

Next, think about getting involved with an organization, volunteering, or starting something yourself that could make a change in that area of interest. This will cause you to get out of your comfort zone. Remember, the discovery of potential rarely occurs within the confines of one's comfortability.

CHAPTER 7

NO SMALL THINKERS ALLOWED

To say that my dad has been one of my biggest inspirations in life would be an understatement. I have been so fortunate to have a father that I could look up to. He has taught me so much about being a man—a *godly* man. As a pastor, speaker, and leader, he has an uncanny ability to encourage people with faith-filled messages of hope and empowerment.

When teaching about leadership, he often tells a story about a professional golfer who visited Saudi Arabia.[1] Some years ago, the king of Saudi Arabia was hosting a private golf tournament and wanted the company of a well-known golf pro from the United States. Both surprised and honored, the golfer kindly agreed. Soon after, the golfer found himself enjoying a refreshing drink as he leaned back in the plush seats of the private plane that the king sent for him.

In the heat of the hot Arabian sun, the king and the golfer played many rounds of golf while sharing stories, enjoying laughs, and feasting on gourmet meals from world-renown chefs. It was an unforgettable week. On the last day, a fleeting frown could be seen on the king's face as the weeklong celebration had come to an end. The king turned toward the golfer as he wondered how to show the golfer his appreciation. "Tell me, what would you like as a token of my appreciation?" the king asked the golfer.

Stepping back in reluctance, the golfer graciously tried to decline his offer, knowing that the expense of that trip was thanks enough. But the king insisted, "You must tell me what kind of gift you want!"

The golfer's voice started to tremble as he attempted to answer, trying to avoid offending the royal family. He blurted out in that moment, almost as if it was instinctual, "A new golf club!"—the quintessential golfer's gift.

As he took the last step onto the plane, the golfer turned around, smiled, and waved goodbye to his royal friends. He looked out of the window at the desert one last time, filled with gratitude as the plane lifted into the air. Reaching for his last few bites of dinner, he pondered what kind of golf club the king might send him. *Would it have expensive materials? Or would it be made with solid gold? Maybe I'll be the only guy in the next tournament to have a club with diamonds on it,* he thought to himself.

He was filled with excitement at the prospect of what it could be.

After the golfer arrived back home, several weeks passed, but there was still no sign of the king's gift. No call from his staff. No text or email. No tracking numbers. Nothing. As he checked the front porch one last time, he wondered to himself, *Did the king forget about my gift?* He dropped his head in disappointment as he closed the front door.

The very next day, however, he heard a knock on the door. Then another knock immediately followed, then another. He opened the door to find a well-dressed gentleman in a three-piece suit holding a large brown envelope. "Hello. How may I help you?" the golfer said. He wasn't expecting anyone (except possibly the delivery man) and thought the visit was a little strange.

"Are you Mr—?" the well-dressed gentleman asked.

"Yes, that's me," the golfer replied. "Sir, I am here to take you to your new golf club." The gentleman extended his arm holding the large brown envelope. Slightly confused, the golfer reluctantly took the envelope and opened it. He stared at the papers in shock as he discovered that he was the new owner of a five hundred-acre golf course estate. The papers were his title deed.

This is a great illustration to help us better understand how God thinks. God doesn't think small—at all. Neither does royalty or royal families. In this story, when the golfer requested a *golf club* he was probably thinking of a single nine iron golf club or a driver. However, the king heard the same request and thought of an entire eighteen-hole golf club estate. Notice how they used the same term, but it meant two different things according to their thinking. The contrasts in their perception and resources made them interpret the same words different ways.

People may think small, but God does not. His thoughts are unlimited in extent, and His plans are eternal in scope. The plans He has for us are *big*, just like He is. He wants us to be courageous enough to accept His thoughts for us. He wants us to go after big dreams. All too often, we shrink the dream God gave us down to the size that we think we can receive. We

> **All too often, we shrink the dream God gave us down to the size that we think we can receive, to the equivalent of our perceived significance.**

scale it down to the equivalent of our perceived significance; a size that's comfortable enough for us to navigate without the assistance of divine intervention or personal maturity. I believe God will allow certain situations to happen in our lives to serve as a catalyst in cultivating our courage and faith. If we see ourselves as small or insignificant, our dreams or aspirations will be small as well. Our dreams often serve as mirrors, helping us understand how we see ourselves.

The Bible makes it plain that God's thoughts and ways are much higher than our human thoughts and natural ways (see Isa. 55:8–9). We serve a supernatural God who has designed us to think like Him because we are fashioned after Him. It is now our responsibility to think on God's level, because that's the type of thinking that pleases Him. A decision about how you think will always lead to a change in how you experience life. That's faith-level thinking. Faith is believing that God is who He says He is in His Word and that He is going to do for you what He said He would do. Faith is being divinely persuaded that the dream He has given you was given to the right person and will be manifested in this earth with His help. This is not just your opportunity; it's your responsibility. As the scripture says, "Without faith it is impossible to please Him…" (Heb. 11:6).

RECEIVING GOD'S ORIGINAL THOUGHTS

As young children, we all dreamed of what we would do when we grew up. Some wanted to become a superstar basketball player, while others wanted to invent some crazy gadget that could teleport them to the moon and back. We all have ideas and concepts about what we want to do, but as we get older, those ideas seem to fade into the background. Our environments, authority figures, and lack of resources may have talked us out of what we previously thought was a great idea. As people grow older, they seem to abandon their dreams like a set of old training wheels.

If I'm describing you right now, don't worry. It's not too late for you. The dream God gave you years ago is still valid. Our dreams are God's original thoughts for us and about us. We just need the proper understanding to accurately perceive God's plans.

I mentioned earlier that I wanted to be a cardiologist. I didn't realize, until many years later, that my dream of becoming a heart surgeon was actually God giving me a clue about my true assignment in full-time ministry. Due to my natural perception, my understanding was limited to my own knowledge and insight. Once I got a clearer understanding of my purpose, everything changed for me, and I was able to passionately pursue the dream God gave me about ministering to the next generation. The whole experience taught me that correctly *interpreting* your God-given purpose is just as important as *knowing* your purpose. It's only God, the Creator of life, who can give you a clear comprehension of your purpose, with keen insight about your unique personality to boot. Don't misinterpret your passion or your assignment, and don't water it down. You must see it through the lens of faith.

When my dad was a boy, he had a recurring dream about people rising from the dead. His father worked at a funeral home for a time while my dad was growing up. In my dad's dream, his father brought home some caskets with bodies in them due to a lack of space at the funeral home. My dad was in his bed, but in the middle of the night, he slowly walked out of his room and into the living room. There he found a room filled with caskets. All was calm until suddenly the caskets flew open and the people in them sat straight up. Then my dad screamed, the hair on the back of his neck standing straight up in terror. It sounds like a zombie movie or a scene from the Michael Jackson "Thriller" music video. Not until he was much older did my dad realize that this recurring dream foreshadowed his calling—to bring people from spiritual death to life by bringing them to Christ.

Here's something to ponder: God has probably spoken to you or showed you His calling and purpose for your life, and you didn't even realize it. Sometimes God is speaking to us and showing us what is to come, but we don't consciously notice it. I declare, from this moment forward, that's going to change. You will have a heightened awareness to discern the divine plans that God has for you.

DON'T FORFEIT YOUR DREAM

If you want to make an impact or live a life of significance, you must dream unapologetically. We are all meant to be dreamers, which is why God often speaks to us through our dreams. This is also why He gave us the capacity to dream by equipping us with an imagination. Your imagination is the rumination station for your dreams. As I mentioned previously, Joseph in the Bible had a few dreams that positioned him as a ruler in his own family and among all the people in his region (see Gen. 37:5–11). When he told his brothers about the dreams he had, it fueled their hatred for him. They already had great disdain for him since he was their father's favorite child.

Joseph's brothers hated him so much that they threw him in a pit, sold him into slavery, took his coat, dipped it in blood, and tricked their father into thinking that Joseph had died. But the power of Joseph's dream was so strong that it moved him from the pit into the royal palace in Egypt in a span of only thirteen years. That was an environment where his dream could be fully expressed.

Here's what we can learn from this example: The more real the dream becomes to you, the more you will see things shift around you. The earth will start to accommodate your dream and make room for its expression and the way you express it—your unique personality.

Even though Joseph's brothers hated him, their hatred couldn't lock him out of his destiny. The haters could not stop him from reaching what God had already prepared for him. The people in his own house couldn't stop Joseph's ascension, and they can't stop yours either. The great news is that your destiny is not up to them. It's up to God and you. No one can stop you from reaching your destiny but you.

But you might ask, "What if people lie about me, frame me for something I didn't do, set me up, or forget about me? Wouldn't that stop me?" Joseph suffered the very same things. He encountered a plot twist in his story as well.

Just as things were going well and Joseph the slave was being promoted in the royal palace, Mrs. Potiphar (the governor's wife) tried to seduce Joseph. When Joseph refused her advances, she lied to her husband and said that Joseph had tried to sexually assault her. Because she lied, Joseph was thrown into prison. But even while he was in prison, he never forgot about the dream God gave him. The change in his environment did not nullify his dream.

Joseph spent *two years* in prison because this woman lied. Imagine the thoughts, feelings, doubts, and frustration he must have felt. But all throughout the story of Joseph, we never get any indication that frustration got the best of him. He refused to let the enemy infiltrate his imagination with bitterness. Two years passed, and Joseph had a divine opportunity to interpret a couple dreams for Pharaoh that no one else could interpret.

After he successfully gave the interpretation, Pharaoh not only released Joseph from prison, but he also promoted him to second-in-command over all of Egypt. From the prison to the palace.

At the end of the story, Joseph's brothers came to get grain from Egypt because of a famine. Joseph was in charge of food distribution. His brothers did not recognize him when they saw him. But when Joseph saw them, he had compassion on them. He knew that part of the assignment God had given him was to help save his family. The apostle Peter reiterates this truth, writing, "Each of you should use whatever gift you have received to serve others, as faithful stewards of God's grace in its various forms" (1 Pet. 4:10 NIV).

Part of the reason God gave you that dream is to help save others. Sometimes God is calling you to help the very people who are saying you can't do it. But you can do it! God has approved you as the best person for the dream He has given you. When a child is being born, a woman goes through labor pains in order to deliver what is inside of her. Usually, conception happens without pain, but much pain and labor is involved in delivery. My point is, many people conceive the dream, but few labor (or work) to deliver on the dream because of the discomfort that comes with it. It's time to labor to bring forth the dream that God placed inside you.

FOR HIS GLORY

I always enjoy going to the airport because of the opportunity to see many unique people from different cultures and backgrounds. I like to imagine what their story might be. As I imagine their stories, it reminds me that we are all gifted in different ways. Some people are gifted externally with an appearance that is very pleasing to the eye. We commonly call it being attractive. I personally believe that my wife is one of those people (as every good husband should believe about his wife).

One day, my wife had gotten ready to go out for the day, and she looked stunning. With a huge grin on my face, I said, "Girl, why are you so fine?!" What she said in response was so simple, but deeply profound.

She smiled at me and said, "Thank you, baby, but it is all for God's glory. I was made attractive to give God glory as His creation and to draw people ultimately to Him." Wow!

Whether you are gifted with good looks, a good sense of humor, superb athletic ability, uncommon creative ability, or the ability to understand people well, one thing is clear: We were all created with these gifts to give God glory. The dream God has given you is designed to glorify Him. In the Bible, the prophet Isaiah states, "Bring all who claim me as their God, for I have made them for my glory. It was I who created them" (Isa. 43:7 NLT).

Ultimately, God gave you your personality to bring Himself glory. Everything about how you were created was made to give God glory. I'm not saying we come into the world as perfect people. That's far from reality. In fact, sin has corrupted our thinking and tainted our proclivities. But when we submit our lives to the Master who is Christ, all that can change. We now have a responsibility to mature. We can and should continue to perfect ourselves, making ourselves better and better every day. But what God has put inside us is prepackaged greatness, waiting to be unpackaged. The

> **As your greatness is revealed, God is glorified.**

purpose of this book is to help you realize that greatness. The scripture says that God will "fulfill his purpose for me" (Ps. 57:2 NLT). The good news is that God does the supernatural work; we just have to obey Him. God is able to do exceedingly abundantly above all that we ask or think, according to His power that works in us (see Eph. 3:20). The power to do whatever you were born to do is already on the inside of you. As your greatness is revealed, God is glorified.

No dream can survive a person who quits. Don't walk away from the dream that is inside of you, because only perseverance can make that dream a reality. What God is going to do through you will benefit many people in society. We need what you carry. We need it more now than perhaps at any other time in history.

The book of Proverbs tells us that if we work hard we will become leaders in the areas God has called us to (see Prov. 12:24). No greatness happens without work. Ultimately, it's not just about the dream; it's about the person you become as a result of pursuing the dream. Just as humankind could not thrive without mothers giving birth to new babies every day, society needs you to give birth to your purpose, your assignment, and your dream through your unique personality.

EXERCISE: VISION CASTING

Create a vision board that represents all the different things you want to accomplish in life. First, find images that visually represent your dreams, goals, and the kind of life you want to live. It might be career, businesses/organizations, family, environments, goods, lifestyle, ministry, artistic endeavors, and so forth. Next, cut out pictures from magazines or news articles or print images that you find online. Affix them to a white poster board and place it somewhere that you can access it weekly or even daily. You can even place one of the scriptures that you identified in the exercises from previous chapters on the board. Make sure to look at it often, giving your mind and heart an opportunity to create the pathway to it. If you want more ideas, do a simple Google search on vision boards.

CHAPTER 8

ARMED FOR THE ASSIGNMENT

Homework and *military*. These are the two words that come to mind when I hear the term *assignment*. Thinking about homework makes most young people cringe, but it is a non-negotiable part of school and college. Regardless of your academic acumen, in order to pass any class and move on to the next class, you must complete various assignments. Although the assignments may be tedious at times, they are designed to facilitate a better understanding of the material.

When I was in school, I found that if I did not do the homework, most times I would not do well on the test. My opportunity to graduate to the next level would be in jeopardy if I did not pass the tests and complete the requirements of the class. Oftentimes, some students in the class didn't want to do the work, but still wanted the benefits that hard work brings. They desired to graduate to the next level but were not willing to put in the work on the current assignment. This kind of thinking can also be described by another word: *entitlement.*

We can draw many conclusions about life from this example. If you want to excel, you must complete the assignments. You have to do the work, even if the work is hard sometimes. Your willingness to participate in the current assignment often prepares the way for you to graduate to the next assignment.

It is extremely important that we are diligent in completing the assignment in front of us, no matter how big or small it is. I'm not talking about scholastic assignments. I'm talking about divine assignments—the plans, dreams, and tasks that God has put in front of you. Writing this book is one of the assignments God gave to me. It has taken me many months and many starts and stops, but I could not abandon the assignment. He also gave me an assignment to create my first online course, called the Winston Leadership Institute, and it was a challenge. I didn't have all of the expertise, but I knew I had to obey God. What assignment or task has God put in your life that He is encouraging you to complete?

My first job as a teenager was working in the facility maintenance department at church. Some parts of the job were very unpleasant, like cleaning toilets and cleaning up messy trash spills. However, the job still needed to get done, even if I did not prefer doing it. Often the most challenging assignments, both in school and in life, are the ones we don't understand. In school, I would sometimes ask the teacher, "Why does this matter? What are we doing this for?" You might be feeling this way right now, trying to figure out the significance of your season. You want to understand how all the details are relevant. But what you need to know is, God has a reason for the assignment, even if you don't understand it. Natural understanding isn't required for obedience to God. Often the discipline that is built as a result of completing assignments or tasks that you neither agree with nor understand is exactly what is needed to facilitate your graduation to the next level. Ironically, discipline exposes both weakness and greatness.

Now let's consider this from a more militant perspective. Soldiers often receive orders, or specific assignments, that they must complete. This requires an even higher level of discipline. I never served in the armed forces, but I'm very familiar with the protocols because my dad was in the United States Air Force for years. I grew up in a military home with an understanding of the importance of assignments and tasks. My dad would tell me, when I was a kid, there were only three acceptable responses when I was asked if I had done a task: *yes sir, no sir,* and *no excuse sir.* If the tasks or assignments were not completed, I would face consequences. Whether we serve in the armed forces or not, God has us all on assignment here on earth. He didn't create us and then say, "Go have fun and do whatever you want!" No. God placed us on earth with a life purpose that includes many different tasks and assignments. Furthermore, He gave each one of us the perfect personality to accomplish our purpose. As a matter of fact, our purpose and personality are interdependent. We may not understand it all now, but in time, it will all make sense.

YOU HAVE EVERYTHING YOU NEED

By the time I was born, my dad was no longer on active duty in the Air Force, but the culture of the military stayed with him. He was a decorated Air Force pilot who fought during the Vietnam War. As a fighter pilot, he wore the uniform provided for him and was equipped with weapons, a fighter jet, and training to fight during the war. While he was serving, the military took care of all his housing costs, food, medical care, compensation needs, and more. The U.S. Air Force did this because they didn't want him to be distracted for one second thinking about anything other than his assignment. They provided everything he needed to make sure he could fulfill the assignment given to him.

The Bible says that we, as Christian believers, are Christ's ambassadors, and God makes His appeal to humankind through us (see 2 Cor. 5:20). An ambassador is a representative of a country who does diplomatic work on behalf of that country. To be an ambassador is to act as an established statesperson or diplomat, a trusted and respected individual who is authorized to speak as a government's representative. You are a representative of God's Kingdom in this world. You are a diplomat of Heaven. You are on assignment and authorized to speak as a representative of the government of God. You are here as an ambassador on earth on behalf of the Kingdom of God to assert God's will over the territory in which you have been given jurisdiction.

When I got this revelation, I finally understood that anything God has given me to do will neither be done in my own power alone nor with my own resources. God has given me an assignment: working on behalf of His Kingdom. So He is obligated to supply everything I need, just as the Air Force would supply everything my dad needed. In fact, God's Word promises us that God will supply all of our needs (see Phil. 4:19). That means that everything I need to complete my assignment is at my disposal. The same goes for you. You are equipped! And part of your equipment is your unique personality supplied by God. This includes not just who you are now, but also who you will evolve into as you complete the divine tasks in front of you.

Everything you need for the mission is already yours. You are not simply on earth to be employed. You have been *deployed*, because you are on assignment. Refuse to believe that just a good job is your end destination or the full extent of your assignment. Ask yourself: *What is the assignment? What's the current task? What's the next thing look like?* God will give you understanding and clarity about your mission in your current assignment.

ASSIGNED TO HELP HUMANITY

When my father was fighting in the Air Force, he was on assignment for the freedom and protection of other people. He willingly had to give up his rights to his own opinions and preferences without prejudice because the mission was not about him. Something more important was at stake, which required the relinquishing of his attitudes. One of the most powerful things I have come to understand about my assignment is that it's not about me. It requires my participation, but my focus must remain on others.

Selfishness will often block the door to the full understanding of one's life purpose. As soon as I start to think it's only about me, it opens the door to confusion. My preferences start contesting with God's direction, obscuring my understanding on where I'm supposed to go and what I'm supposed to do. But when I take a moment to refocus, allowing myself to align with God's objectives first, I know how to move forward. Not only do I know where to go and what to do, but now I have power to advance, take over, and win in my assigned territory. When we team up with God, we will never lose.

In the Bible, right after Solomon became king, God asked him what he wanted and promised that whatever he asked would be granted to him (see 1 Kings 3:3–14). Solomon asked for wisdom so that he could judge God's people correctly. Since Solomon decided to ask

> **Our assignment, purpose, and personality were given to us with the main goal of helping humanity.**

for something that would benefit others, not just himself, God decided to give him what he asked for and also make him the richest person alive. Solomon was rewarded for discovering the key: It's not just about me. The same goes for us. Our assignment, purpose, and personality were given to us with the main goal of helping humanity.

As I mentioned in an earlier chapter, God will equip you with what you need for the benefit of others because it is necessary for your assignment. If you feel like you are weak in an area, submit that weakness to God. The apostle Paul made this plain to us when he recorded these words God spoke to him:

> ..."*My grace is always more than enough for you, and my power finds its full expression through your weakness.*" *So I will celebrate my weaknesses, for when I'm weak I sense more deeply the mighty power of Christ living in me. So I'm*

> *not defeated by my weakness, but delighted! For when I feel my weakness and endure mistreatment—when I'm surrounded with troubles on every side and face persecution because of my love for Christ—I am made yet stronger. For my weakness becomes a portal to God's power* (2 Corinthians 12:9-10 TPT).

Paul learned not to rely on his own strength, knowledge, information, education, skills, power, or the accolades of others, even though he could have. Paul was one of the most well-educated men at that time, yet still he experienced the pain of weakness.

When I feel weak or inadequate, then I say, "God, it's got to be all of You. I trust *You* to empower me." When you take this attitude toward your weaknesses, *God will equip you beyond your weaknesses for the benefit of others.* As I stated before, I didn't like public speaking, and I wasn't very good at it. But God was able to equip me beyond my weaknesses in order to bless many others because I trusted Him. The Bible says,

> *If anyone speaks, let him speak as the oracles of God. If anyone ministers, let him do it as with the ability which God supplies, that in all things God may be glorified through Jesus Christ...* (1 Peter 4:11).

God has equipped you in the same way so that you can be a blessing to others and complete your mission.

ABLE + AVAILABLE

God is not just looking for ability, because He knows where your abilities lie. He made you, and He formed you. He knew you before you were in your mother's womb. Nothing in us is hidden from God. What God looks for is *availability*—those who will say *yes* to Him with their gifts, skills, and abilities. Those who will say *yes* to doing what God has called them to do and *yes* to the plan of God to help humankind.

God has placed great potential inside you, and He has glorious plans for you, but you have the option to leave it dormant. God has given us free will to make choices. You can choose not to follow the plan of God. You can allow doubt and unbelief to keep you from your purpose. I grew up in church, sat in many pews, and attended many church services, but sitting in the pews alone won't make anything happen. *God's plan doesn't automatically happen in our lives; We have to choose it.* We have to choose to be used by God and move past our fears, doubts, and insecurities. Refusing to believe that God could use somebody like you could rob you of seeing God's supernatural power at work.

God cannot do mighty works in your life if you choose not to believe. But all things become possible for those who believe in God. When Jesus ministered to the people, His ability didn't change, but the people's belief dictated the flow of power coming from Him. He even said to two blind men who were asking to have their sight restored, "Become what you believe" (Matt. 9:29 MSG).

God is willing and ready to use you and your unique personality. He will do a miraculous work through your authenticity. He is ready to use you right now. The question is, what are you doing with your ability? Are you stepping out?

> **The power of God will flow in your life when you are obedient to Him.**

Are you stepping up? Are you taking advantage of those opportunities? Are you setting goals or taking any risks? God might be calling you to start an organization, business, or ministry. It doesn't matter if you are sixteen or sixty-five. Start now! If God says to do something, do it when He tells you to do it. God's power isn't hindered because of your age or background. The abilities and gifts in you are not validated because of degrees and education. The vision God gave you isn't waiting on you to have a certain amount of money in the bank. In the Bible, God often calls people to do great things despite what they don't have. Follow God, step by step. It doesn't matter if people don't think you're qualified. Step up anyway. Tell God and show God that you are available.

Here is the secret: The power of God will flow in your life when you are obedient to Him. *Your obedience is the best way to prove to God that you are not just able; you are available.* But your disobedience can hinder God's work. Ending world hunger, stopping mass shootings, improving conditions in our inner cities, creating government accountability, eliminating systemic poverty, closing the wealth gap—God has solutions for all of the world's problems. But it takes authentic people receiving divine wisdom to discover permanent solutions. Everything that you need to complete your assignment is at your disposal. Your personality, creativity, aptitudes, passions, insights, solutions, and intelligence are your equipment. Rest assured, the equipment you have is the exact equipment that you need for the mission at hand. It's time to win the battle!

EXERCISE: THE STORY BEHIND THE STORY

Think of a well-known, influential person you really admire. They don't necessarily need to be in the industry in which you desire to succeed, or the industry that you are currently in. They just need to be someone you admire. Take some time to research their story. Read their biography and listen to their interviews. Gain an understanding of their story, especially some of the hardships and challenges they overcame. Can you see how their struggles helped them develop into the person they became?

CHAPTER 9

PREPARATION IS PURPOSE

Several years ago, I discovered a place that would become very dear to my heart: Mastro's Steakhouse. It has become one of my favorite steakhouse spots in Chicago. I don't know what Mastro does to make his food so delicious, but it is wonderful. The whole dining experience is a masterpiece. The truth is, I can count on one hand how many times I have been there, but it still doesn't stop me from recommending it to anyone looking for a fancy (and expensive) fine dining experience in Chicago.

Whether you enjoy dining at home or at a fancy restaurant, all good meals have this in common: They require a certain amount of preparation. After deciding what to cook, meal prep starts with a trip to the grocery store—or ordering grocery delivery from the comfort of your couch. No one can cook a really good meal without first gathering all the proper ingredients during the preparation phase. This phase of the meal is separate from the finished product, when the food is finally ready for consumption. The preparation phase is important, but it's not the *purpose* of the meal. The purpose of the meal is to feed people. *Preparation is necessary to accomplish the purpose.*

Many chefs and food connoisseurs say the best way to enjoy a steak is cooked medium, but I prefer mine a little more cooked, on the medium-well side. In college, I had a professor who spent the better part of class one day trying to convince us that we should be eating our steaks as rare as we can get them. No thanks. Everyone is entitled to their own opinion, of course. But to me, that sounds terrible. The few times when I've ordered a steak and it came out even close to rare, I immediately sent it back, because the way the steak was prepared did not appeal to me.

The same thing happens during the *preparation phase* of your purpose. Your preparation phase can be compared to a hot oven that is preparing you to be received and consumed. Right now, God is preparing you to be the most palatable to the culture or people that He has assigned you to influence. We can think of it as a sort of development.

The scripture says, "To everything there is a season, a time for every purpose under heaven" (Eccles. 3:1).

Timing is very important to God. He knows when it's your time. He knows when it's your season. He knows when you have the development necessary to be received well. If you try to leave the preparation phase too soon, you will go underdeveloped, risking the same fate as the undercooked steak. You might be *what* was needed, but not delivered the *way* others needed it. Preparation is purposeful and necessary, and it is a process.

Preparation is part of living out your purpose every day. It's not something that you only pursue after college or well into your thirties. Jesus was a carpenter before He traveled and ministered. While Jesus was a carpenter, God was preparing Him for the next phase of His purpose to be perfectly expressed. Jesus was working out His potential. He was developing His brand of greatness. He was growing in His own grace.

Jesus was a carpenter by trade, but that job in carpentry didn't encapsulate His full calling. It was simply a season and an expression of His purpose at that stage of life. This means you can be living out your purpose while working at a job down the street at XYZ company, even if you have a ministry calling. You can be discovering your greatness while you are clocking in every morning at the job or sitting in class at school. You can undergo development in obscurity. Remember, something inside you is always being developed (if you are willing to participate).

Jesus did not do anything without purpose. God equipped Him before He went into His next season. According to the Bible, Jesus learned wisdom, among other things, during those seasons (see Luke 2:52). Jesus was not living outside of purpose before ministry. He was perfect in every way, living a sinless life, obeying the Father until the very end. Many people think of purpose as a singular experience on the linear timeline of sequential events. But Jesus' earthly example seems to debunk that logic. Maybe, instead, our perspective is inaccurate. I believe Jesus was not living outside of purpose for thirty years. *He was living inside of preparation.* Purpose and preparation are interconnected. They have a symbiotic relationship in which one is always making room for the

> **"Purpose and preparation are interconnected."**

other. Preparation leads to expressions of purpose. That then leads back to more preparation for a greater expression of purpose, accomplishing God's will in superior measure each time.

A great Thanksgiving Day meal may only take thirty minutes to eat, but it can take several days to prepare. The preparation is absolutely necessary to facilitate the purpose. I heard someone say this powerful statement, and I will never forget it: "You can be anointed, but not announced." Some of us are looking to be announced, searching for the validation of our significance, but we have not finished the preparation phase for what the Lord has planned. God has promised that He will exalt you in due time if you humble yourself before Him (see 1 Pet. 5:6). That means we must submit and subscribe to His method of training. *Preparation is still a part of the meal, even if no one has come to sit down at the table yet.* Sometimes that can be the hardest challenge—wondering if anyone will come and sit to eat the meal once it is prepared. That is where you must have faith, trusting that God knows what He's doing. I believe He's preparing people even now to sit at your table and partake of your gifts.

The Bible says, "For you have been called for this purpose, since Christ also suffered for you, leaving you an example for you to follow in His steps" (1 Pet. 2:21 NASB). Since Jesus walked according to purpose and spent years in preparation, we can expect a similar preparation process. Your preparation doesn't just come *before* you start fulfilling your life's purpose. Your preparation is *part* of living out your purpose.

TOUGH SKIN FOR THE JOB

When God first gave me a clear understanding of my purpose, I didn't immediately jump into a pulpit. I wasn't trying to find every opportunity to get on somebody else's stage. The fact that I had a ministry calling on my life didn't mean I was prepared at that moment to be able to minister to the needs of the people. I had to hear God's direction and allow Him to guide me through my process. The Lord led me to get more training, so I enrolled at the Graduate School of Theology and Ministry (Seminary) at Oral Roberts University in Tulsa, Oklahoma. That was part of my preparation.

Early in ministry, I learned how to love people, and I continue to grow in loving others day by day. As social media has grown in popularity, some unpleasant things have grown along with it. People can sometimes be very cruel behind their screens when they are commenting on my father's messages. It was hard to take for the first year or so. My patience was tested many times as I helped manage some of our digital and social media. I typed and then deleted many replies. I wanted so badly to come to my father's defense, especially because I know the heart behind his teaching. But I had to learn that some people want to discredit you and discourage you. I had to learn that some people don't want to hear the truth. Some people are not interested in being considerate; they just want to express their own opinions. But I have to love them anyway.

Some people won't agree with you, your expression, your interpretation, or your opinion. And that's okay. You can't control what others say or do, but you can always control how you respond. I learned that every ignorant comment doesn't need to be answered. That was part of my preparation process. I had to master having tough skin and self-control. I had to learn how to love people even if they weren't acting very loveable.

If I hadn't gone through the process in developing my *love muscle*, when I came to the bigger stages with more influence and visibility, I would not have known how to handle unpleasant responses. It's all part of the process. My purpose is full-time ministry, but God won't elevate me into failure. He develops me until I am ready to handle what is next. He helps me work on my deficiencies, and He will help you work on yours too. What is God asking you to master in this season? You will need it later, I promise.

Often, as in my case, preparation can look like growing in love. For others, preparation may be focused on recalibrating self-image. For some, it might involve growing in faith and trusting in God. Others will grow in character, integrity, caring for the needs of others, managing money, organization, resilience, and other skills. The point is: Everybody has an area that needs preparation before elevation.

PREPARING THE PRODUCT

Diamonds hold great value in our society and are highly sought after, even though they're made from common substances like carbon, dirt, and natural elements. Even synthetic diamonds are made from a very common material: lead (the same lead you find in cheap #2 pencils). These common substances produce something of value when the proper process takes place. Extreme heat and immense pressure bring the common raw materials together to produce something beautiful and very expensive. The preparation can be used to assess value. Without preparation, the proper value of a thing is not known or realized.

> **Without preparation, the proper value of a thing is not known or realized.**

The preparation you are going through, which will make you into the finished product, is necessary to bring out the best in you. But preparation looks different for different people. As I stated earlier, preparation helps us grow as we refine our character. These are some common areas where many of us need preparation in order to step into our purpose:

- Learning patience in times when you feel overlooked and unheard
- Choosing obedience/submission to God rather than what seems easy
- Understanding how to hear God's voice
- Growing your knowledge in the specific area that you're pursuing
- Surviving failure

- Using your faith
- Growing your skills in certain areas
- Learning to love and forgive people
- Submitting to authority
- Recalibrating your self-image
- Operating with honesty and integrity
- Building character
- Eliminating the wrong relationships to make room for the right ones
- Exercising good stewardship over resources
- Learning to value what is important
- Exercising selflessness
- Growing in humility and showing honor
- Using good judgment in decision making
- Working with others and putting the team first
- Transitioning to a new job or new location (flexibility)
- Exercising resilience
- Knowing how to trust God beyond what you can see

When I think of the oven of preparation, I often think of faithfulness. As the old saying goes, "If you can't stand the heat, then get out of the kitchen." Many times when the heat is on we're tempted to leave in order to get the pressure off of us. Only people who are faithful and know what is ahead can stand the pressure of the preparation phase. While you may not be able to control the talents and abilities God gives you, you can control your willingness to be faithful in how you develop them. *God will not force preparation on you. He will only offer you the opportunity to get prepared; you can decide to take it or not.*

In the New Testament, Jesus told a parable of three servants who received different amounts of money or talents from their master (see Matt. 25:14–30). One servant received five talents, another received two talents, and the last one received one talent. The servants with the five talents and the two talents both acted responsibly and were able to double their money. Their master said to them, "Well done, my good and faithful servant. You have been faithful in handling this small amount, so now I will give you many more responsibilities…" (Matt. 25:23 NLT). He called them faithful because of their willingness to be responsible over and grow the talents he gave to them. Their display of good stewardship led to positive recognition.

When we are responsible over the talents or abilities God gives us, He counts us as faithful. Endurance in the

> **While you may not be able to control the talents and abilities God gives you, you can control your willingness to be faithful.**

preparation phase is one of the ways we can display our faithfulness to God. In this way, He sees who is ready to be promoted to the next level of increase, influence, and exposure. If you are looking for God to promote you, ask yourself, "Am I being as faithful and fruitful as possible where I'm at right now?" Faithfulness is a signal that you are just about done and ready to come out of the oven of preparation. *Ding!* It's time to go to the next level.

DOING MORE WITH LESS

In the days before we had advanced computers, people had to edit film and music by hand. This involved taking actual recorded tape or developed film, cutting it to remove or insert the part in question, and then splicing the tape or film together for use. The parts that were cut out would end up, at least temporarily, on the cutting room floor. The cutting room floor is where certain parts of a film wind up during editing for one reason or another. They could be bloopers or bad takes. Some scenes may not have added value to the film or fit the overall storyline, so they were eliminated from the film.

I use this as an example because God is the director of our lives, and He is the author of our story. At times, in the midst of preparation, we can feel like things are being stripped away or edited out. It could be relationships, jobs, opportunities, or even resources that abruptly come to an end. Perhaps at the beginning of the week you felt like you had it all together, only to have everything fall apart by the weekend. Don't worry. You are not alone. And God is not punishing you. But He will use these situations to strengthen you.

I'm certainly not saying that God is the cause of trauma, sicknesses, death, loss, or tragedies. The Bible states that God cannot tempt anyone with evil (see James 1:13), and His will for us is to live an abundant life (see John 10:10) despite the effects of evil in our world. God is not the author of death and destruction, but He will use adverse conditions to bring something beautiful out of us in the midst of unexplainable hardship.

God, through His infinite wisdom, will never waste your pain when you submit it to Him. Sometimes your greatest pains end up becoming your greatest strengths. That's the redeeming power of God. God requires development, and He's always developing you, even in seasons of distress and hardship. He accepts you for who you are, but loves you too much to let you stay that way. He's editing your life to help you become better and stronger.

I believe in growing stronger. As a matter of fact, I like to work out and exercise often, keeping my natural body strong. I worked as a personal trainer for a few years before I went into ministry, and I have a bachelor's degree in health and exercise science. People would hire me to help them get into shape. I would always tell clients that muscles can only grow back bigger and stronger if you break them down and tear the fibers first. Since Jesus is the author and perfecter of our faith, I like to say that Jesus is our faith personal trainer (see Heb. 12:2). He is here to help our spirits get strong. We just have to follow His lead.

He is in charge of your life development, but you are responsible for it. You have to subscribe to it. You have to show up for this development. Situations and scenarios will come in life that you can't control, but God will use them to build you up and equip you for your purpose. With God's help, you are becoming the purest version of yourself—purifying your greatness.

Furthermore, God often chooses those who know they need Him to succeed. God has chosen you to go through this process. Don't be in a hurry to leave the phase of preparation. It's hard for God to use and develop those who are trusting in their own strength. Trusting in your own strength is trusting in yourself more than you trust in God. Instead, trust God and stick with Him. The apostle Paul writes:

> *Remember, dear brothers and sisters, that few of you were wise in the world's eyes or powerful or wealthy when God called you. Instead, God chose things the world considers foolish in order to shame those who think they are wise. And he chose things that are powerless to shame those who*

are powerful. God chose things despised by the world, things counted as nothing at all, and used them to bring to nothing what the world considers important (1 Corinthians 1:26–28 NLT).

THE BEST IS YET TO COME

God is preparing to use you in a special way. That is why He is taking His time preparing you and editing out anything that shouldn't be in your life or heart. He is perfecting you for a purpose. A life of purpose is filled with times and seasons of preparation. In fact, purpose is always before you, waiting for you to encounter it through the everyday decisions you make. But you will have to submit your will to God, hear His voice, and get instructions from Him on how to move forward. Take your cue from Jesus; He went through thirty years of preparation, for three years of ministry, that led to three hours of destiny, so that we could be saved, eternally. Where you are right now is all part of the plan. God knows your future and is equipping you for your path.

EXERCISE: IT'S GROW TIME

Let's be purposeful about preparation. Identify something that could facilitate your growth in this season. It could be enrolling in an online course, volunteering to lead something at work or church, accepting a work assignment, getting involved in a small group, starting a home Bible study, engaging in a community project, going back to school to finish your degree program, starting a business/side hustle, or something else. Decide to enroll in something that will strategically help you grow beyond your own comfort level.

CHAPTER 10

COURAGE: THE POWER TO BE TRANSPARENT

Sometimes dreams in the night can be so vivid and realistic that it takes some time to figure out whether it was real life or just a dream. I can think of multiple times when the feelings expressed in my dreams were so strong that they continued when I woke up. If something bad happened in the dream, the same feelings of anxiety tried to grip me once I awakened. Sometimes I have even had to ask my wife if what I dreamed actually happened.

This is exactly how fear tries to operate in our lives. Fear is like a dream. It's not real, but it tries to convince you of its reality. It uses your imagination against you. Fear paints a bleak picture that seems so real that you start to question yourself and what you know to be reality.

Fear is something that, if gone unchecked, will poison your thinking and infect your future aspirations.

Fear tries to sabotage your progress by forecasting your failure. Many people are unaware that their greatest fear might actually be *being themselves.* It is commonly said that courage is not the absence of fear, but the strength to move past it. Many people settle for where they are in life because it is safe, comfortable, and familiar. Some people fear being authentic. But this doesn't have to be your story. Striving to reach your destiny is going to take great courage in the midst of uncertainty. Good thing you are a courageous person!

The Bible says, "For God has not given us a spirit of fear, but of power and of love and of a sound mind" (2 Tim. 1:7). Fear does not come from God. Fear comes from the devil, and he uses it to torment people. But when God is with you, you have nothing to fear. God's love works as an agent of protection. You are His child, the apple of His eye (see Zech. 2:8). He is keeping careful watch over you. Fear says, "I can't. I won't." Faith says, "I can, and I will." Choose to be a person of faith and courage.

The word *courage* comes from two Latin words: *cor-* meaning heart, and *-age* which has several meanings— process, collection, cumulative result of, place of, rank, or charge.[1] We can define courage in several ways, but the definition I like best is the one Brené Brown gave in her TEDx talk: "Telling the story of who you are with your whole heart."[2] That's courage. Being your authentic self, especially among a group of strangers, can be intimidating. The thought of "letting people in" can be scary to some, because it takes courage to allow people to see the real you. But it's both empowering and liberating to be the person you are most familiar with: *you*. Remember, you have God's DNA flowing inside you. If God made all of us in His image and likeness, then our very existence and the use of our uniqueness, creativity, attributes, and abilities is telling the story of who *He* is.

A FUTURE FAVORITE

Being who God made you to be takes an abundance of courage. Allowing the full expression of your personality to shine through is no easy task. In today's culture, it is so easy to be like someone else because we are constantly given so much access to people's lives. In our society, we put so much emphasis on being ready (through things like training and education), rather than being dauntless. It's easy and quite tempting to just replicate what someone else is doing, but the results of that are limited. It also robs the world of the chance to see the full expression of your purpose through your unique personality. Whether in an organization, business, church, artistic expression, media, or sport, the world is waiting for you to do it in your unique way.

We may be facing many challenges in our world, but God planned your birth as the perfect response to something He saw coming in the future. The potency of that solution can only be delivered through the authenticity of your approach. God knows the answer for every problem, and He brings someone into the earth to accomplish this goal. A solution exists for every issue we encounter. Just remember, *every solution has a face.* One of those faces is yours.

Maybe you don't feel like you are that smart. Maybe you feel incapable of solving important problems. That may be how you feel based on past experiences, but you were born brilliant. You simply need the right environment and guidance to expose your specific brand of brilliance. It's critically important to God (and society) that you be your true self.

Let's say you have a favorite place to grab a cheeseburger. Many places serve cheeseburgers. Why do you prefer that particular place? It's because you like the way *they* do it. Other places may do a fine job making burgers, but it's just not the same as your favorite place. That's the way you should think about your unique ability. Other people will be able to do what you can do (because they have a similar purpose), but delivering it through your unique personality makes it something very special. The way you do what you do will make you someone's

> **You are someone's future favorite just waiting to be discovered.**

favorite. Authenticity is always interesting, even if you feel like you are not. As I mentioned earlier, you are someone's future favorite just waiting to be discovered. However, no one can discover this if you remain in hiding. All of this takes courage, and it starts with you and how you value yourself. If you value what you have, you will understand the importance of sharing it with the world.

PARALYSIS

Courage is the strength to move forward in the face of adversity. Even when conditions aren't perfect, you can refuse to be paralyzed by uncertainty. Fear of rejection and fear of failure can often be paralyzing. Paralysis can be provoked through tough circumstances that induce fear. Other times, an imagined scenario, completely fabricated by your mind, can trap you in fear. Biblical principles and psychology together tell us that the more you see a picture in your mind, the more real it becomes to you.

God designed us to live from the inside out. This means that when the picture inside of you becomes more real to you than the reality you see on the outside, you will go in the direction of the picture. So if the picture inside of you is a negative one, you will go in a negative direction. These are the "imaginations" the apostle Paul says we must cast down (see 2 Cor. 10:5

KJV). For example, people who fear flying have imagined the grim picture of what could happen to them if they get on a plane. Even if it's a nice day with clear blue skies, the mental picture is still the same. So is the action that follows. They are stuck on the ground because of their thoughts. Fear leads to paralysis, and the decision not to fly as a result.

I remember one ordinary night at home with my dad when I was about nine years old. We were downstairs in the living room, and I decided to go upstairs to get something from my room. I ran up the carpeted stairs one after the other, forgetting to turn on the light switch in my haste. Suddenly, something quickly ran across the hallway, from my bedroom into the laundry room. I saw a quick flash of light just four steps away from my location on the stairs. It was only a distance of several feet from one room to the other. It was so quick that if I had blinked I would have missed it. I stood there dazed and confused, questioning my own sanity, but I just knew I had seen something.

Since my dad and I were the only two people home, I wasn't sure what or who could be running through the house. I believed in angels, but I had never had an encounter with one. I hoped it was an angel I saw, but I was fearful that it might have been something else. So what did I do? I'd like to tell you that I did something brave, but I did not. I did absolutely nothing. I was frightened. I stood right there on the staircase for almost an hour. Fear had literally paralyzed me. I could not move forward because of what I had seen. It made me feel uncertain about what was going to happen next. I wanted to move, but I literally felt like my feet were glued to the floor. I could not move.

Finally, I decided to take courage and not stay there any longer. (The courage probably stemmed from having to go to the bathroom and not being able to hold it any longer.) I went down the stairs, grabbed my bat from the garage, and then went back up the stairs, going from room to room like a vigilante soldier (kind of like my favorite superhero, Batman). Thankfully, I didn't find anything, and everything was fine for the rest of the night. Could it have been an angel? Possibly. But that experience taught me how paralyzing fear can be.

Today, some people live their lives frozen in fear, just like I was, on those stairs, years ago. It makes them sit on the sidelines of life, only existing and never living life to the fullest. My friend, you can't achieve your destiny sitting on the sidelines. You have to make up your mind to move forward. Fear can be described as false evidence appearing real (F.E.A.R.). The stories that fear tells you are full of false evidence, and those stories always have a bad ending. You must make up your mind not to agree with those stories. Rather, let God show you the story He is writing for you, and agree with Him. That's faith; agreeing with God.

PERFECTIONIST PARALYSIS

As imperfect people, we can sometimes find it challenging to move past our deficiencies. In the pursuit of destiny and purpose, this is another kind of paralysis—*perfectionist paralysis*. Perfectionism, in psychology terms, is a "personality trait characterized by a person's striving for flawlessness and setting excessively high performance standards, commonly accompanied by overly critical self-evaluations."[3] Paralysis can be defined as "immobility or powerlessness."[4]

People who deal with perfectionist paralysis become immobile due to their desire to achieve perfection before they make a move. In their quest for perfection, they become completely stuck. But God doesn't need you to be perfect in order to work through you. In fact, God specializes in using imperfect people, and He can work through you in the same way. However, you can never perfect something that

> **God specializes in using imperfect people, and He can work through you in the same way.**

you refuse to start working on. If you wait until everything is perfect to do, start, or finish what God has placed in your heart, you may never complete it. The enemy will always preoccupy you with obstacles to deter you, but don't fall for that trap. Make up your mind to get *moving*. A great destiny awaits you. Refuse to get stuck trying to be perfect.

FEAR OF FAILURE

I mentioned earlier that fear tries to poison your progress by forecasting your failure. Having courage doesn't mean fear doesn't exist; it means God is strengthening you with His power. He is empowering you to move past the situations and circumstances that previously had you bound. Sometimes what we think is failure is really God reorganizing our lives and reshaping our priorities to get us in alignment with His divine timing and direction. Failure is never final unless you decide to quit.

I heard one man say that fear of failure is the greatest enemy of success. Maybe you have experienced a failed business, failed marriage, failed attempt at college, or some other failure, but God is with you, and He will lead you as you start over. Maybe the timing was off, or maybe the right people weren't involved yet. Maybe you didn't have the right perspective yet. I don't know your situation, but I do know that God plans to prosper you. Failure can become a catalyst toward success, if you let it. It's all in the way you perceive it.

If you have failed in the past, I have good news for you—your future is more important than your past. Don't ever live in a way that is more committed to your past than to your future. The Bible advises us to forget about the past and focus on what is ahead (see Phil. 3:13). It's never too late to begin again. Every time you try again you are one step closer to success. I like what the famous inventor, Thomas Edison (who owns over 1,000 patents), said, "Our greatest weakness lies in giving up. The most certain way to succeed is to try just one more time."[5]

FEAR OF REJECTION

Have you ever heard a guitar or piano being tuned? It sounds bad when the different keys sound too much alike or are out of tune. The piano sounds best when all of the keys sound uniquely different and distinct. Only then can a person correctly play and compose music on it. Fear tries to tell us our differences won't be accepted. In reality, it's our differences that will make us most celebrated. It's our differences that are most valuable. World-class athletes, artists, and entertainers are celebrated because they bring something new or different to the world. They expressed their gift in a way that no one had ever seen.

You may have had somebody tell you that you're not smart, you don't have the right look, you don't have good ideas, or you don't have what it takes to play the part. You may have felt rejected or abandoned. Because of those negative experiences, you may have decided to hide in a shell. The real you has retracted back so that you can feel safe and avoid ridicule. Unfortunately, many times people make comments like that because they too are suffering and feel inadequate. They project those feelings of inadequacy onto others, trying to make them feel insecure as well. All those feelings of inadequacy, rejection, and jealousy only work to convince us that we are not the right people to pursue our dreams. The book of Proverbs reminds us that fearing the opinions of others will cause us to stagnate: "Fearing people is a dangerous trap, but trusting the Lord means safety" (Prov. 29:25 NLT).

> **It's our differences that will make us most celebrated. It's our differences that are most valuable.**

Today is a good day to put an end to fear-based thinking. You can decide that everything will change starting right now. The resolve to change is the first decision you must make in pursuit of courage. It's easy to stay the same. If changing were easy, everybody would do it. But it's not. The good news is, God doesn't expect you to do it on your own. He will help you through the change process. He specializes in bringing the best out of people. He's a transformation expert and knows what is needed for your metamorphosis to take place. The exercise at the end of this chapter lists some ways you can take courage.

Remember, courage is like a muscle: The more you exercise it, the stronger you become. Courage is an agent of empowerment. Courage gives you the freedom to be yourself. It takes courage to be transparent. Some people are natural-born risk takers, so it is easier for them to step out in the midst of uncertainty. Others are analyzers and have to assess all of the risk first. If it seems too risky, they tend to back off. No matter which temperament you have, you have to be willing to take the risk. Some of the best things in life will be risky: starting a new job, moving to a new state, getting married, going away to college, planting a church, starting a business, changing careers, having kids, and so forth.

Life is full of big decisions filled with uncertainty about the unknown. These decisions have the potential to change your life for the better. The more we move toward our fears, facing them head-on, the smaller they become. So, take courage. You will live the best of life only when you decide to live authentically.

EXERCISE: MOVE FORWARD IN THE FACE OF FEAR

Executing these simple steps will help you take courage:

- Do something that you feel like you wouldn't or couldn't do before. It could be as simple as facing a phobia or doing something you've been putting off due to fear.

- Afterward, ask yourself, "Was that as bad as I thought it would be?"

- Build a good support system around yourself. Let people who truly know and love you affirm you.

- Pray and ask God for courage; then listen. Write down what God is speaking to you, and find a scripture to anchor your faith.

- Remember that God is leading your process and knows more about your ability than you do, because He created you.

CHAPTER 11

DON'T DARE COMPARE: MAINTAINING YOUR VALUE

Neil Harris was a high school English teacher. For years, he enjoyed teaching and watching students learn and grow. But during his years in the school system, he also noticed various deficiencies. It seemed like a lot of the information that builds value in students for career success was not being taught in the curriculum. Apathy was growing in the student body. The students just didn't seem to care much about what the books taught because it didn't relate to them. They couldn't see how knowing the information would help them live the life they wanted. Simply put, to them it seemed like pointless information.

Neil realized that if he wanted students to value education, he had to first get them to pay attention. He wanted students to get real, applicable life skills in the classroom. The problem was, they could barely pay attention because they were so stressed out about not having enough food to eat, not having enough money for basic life expenses, and other poverty-related issues. Neil decided that in order to be most effective, he would have to go outside the walls of formal education. He left his teaching job to start a staffing company called Prestigious Placement in Memphis, Tennessee.[1]

Neil decided to model his company after the system used by many entertainers and athletes. Just as these individuals hire agents to advance their careers, Neil figured he would act as an agent for young people to help them to get regular jobs. Sports agents invest in young athletes to help them advance their careers because the agents see value in their potential. Agents identify potential on the front-end, invest in their development in the middle, and get paid handsomely on the back end for all of their investment. And that's exactly what Neil decided to do. He sees the value in others, teaches them the skills and information that will help them value themselves, and then provides resources necessary to keep them going in the right direction. Neil says, "We are offering to lower-income people what's been offered to higher-income people for years now—an agent. As agents, we believe in our clients and invest in them." Neil decided to become a career agent who drafted kids out of high school and helped them build a career in logistics. During this process, as a byproduct, he started to see the self-images of the young people transform.

Neil decided to make education and logistics just as valuable as sports and entertainment, investing in these young adults just like a sports agent would. His company helps to solve real-life issues, like giving gas cards to those who don't have enough money to put gas in their car. They even send a car to pick up anyone who doesn't have transportation to work. If a client needs dental work, the company will cover it. If the client needs food, the company will provide it. As long as the young person is still going to work, Prestigious Placement will continue to invest in him or her. On the back-end, Prestigious Placement gets a return on their investment once people get back on their feet. That's their business model. They don't want anything to distract their clients from moving forward.

Neil says that by doing business this way, they help their people find their purpose while instilling principles that make them more valuable to all of their corporate partners. One of the best parts is that they teach their clients about God, instilling biblical principles that will help them be a success from the inside out.

Neil teaches them how to have the correct self-image. Your self-image, or inner image, is how you honestly see yourself. Your self-image dictates where you can go in life. In fact, your self-image will take you to the place where it can express itself the most. Your self-image also serves as the filter through which you process every idea, thought, word, and action. If that self-image is not calibrated correctly to who God says you are, you will find yourself working against your purpose. Neil knew that, and decided that training young people to have the correct self-image was one of the best ways for them to avoid self-sabotage.

Years ago, while working in the schools, Neil saw this self-image deficit in the students and decided to make a career change. This minority-owned company has grown tremendously over the years in both size and reputation. In 2004, Neil received a Lifetime Achievement Award from Walmart for excellence in logistics. In 2017, they were recognized as one of the best employment agencies in Memphis. They have gone from just a few employees to over five thousand. It all started with a vision to build value in others and help them see the value in themselves—to help students understand that it's not about how we *compare* to one another, but rather how we *value* each other.

BEWARE OF THE TEMPTATION TO COMPARE

In our culture today, we are tempted with countless opportunities to compare ourselves with others. We live in a highlight-reel culture. We can see everyone's achievements and fun times on social media, but none of their struggles or behind-the-scenes shortcomings. This can leave you wondering, *What's wrong with me?*

Why is my life such a struggle? The Word of God says it's not wise to compare yourself with others (see 2 Cor. 10:12). Comparison will make you focus on what you don't have (or in the case of social media, on an artificially manufactured lifestyle). Eventually, it will cause you to feel inadequate.

A very close friend once said, "Never compare yourself to someone else, because you'll always discover you're not them." It's a simple and profoundly true statement. Comparison kills confidence. The moment we wish we had the gift that someone else has, we automatically devalue our own gift.

The enemy often uses comparison as bait so that over time being yourself becomes less and less attractive to you. Then you find yourself trapped in a prison you can't get out of, because you can't escape yourself. The enemy doesn't want you to be

> **The enemy often uses comparison as bait so that over time being yourself becomes less and less attractive to you.**

who you are, because being yourself is powerful. God made you unique, in your own skin, for your own purpose.

Imagine you gave two different toys to two different children. The first child got a toy that walks around, and the second child got a toy that lights up. If the first child compared his toy to the other child's toy, then he might start to devalue what he had because it's not as bright. I'm a father of four children, and sometimes this happens in my house. One of my kids will ask, "Why didn't I get what he has?" My answer to that is the same as what the Father tells us—be grateful for your own gift, and you will find much more happiness and fulfillment. I'm sure most parents can relate.

You will never be able to find peace within yourself if you don't follow the guidelines for regulating your thinking. I like what Joel Osteen, pastor of Lakewood Church in Houston, Texas, says, "Don't focus on your weakness; focus on your God…When you think positive, excellent thoughts, you will be propelled towards greatness."[2] *You can't think negatively about yourself and be at peace with yourself at the same time.* The apostle Paul tells us how to maintain a healthy thought life:

> *So keep your thoughts continually fixed on all that is authentic and real, honorable and admirable, beautiful and respectful, pure and holy, merciful and kind. And fasten your thoughts on every glorious work of God, praising him always. Follow the example of all that we have imparted to you and the God of peace will be with you in all things* (Philippians 4:8–9 TPT).

I believe the happiest people in life are those who have decided to fully accept who they are and what they are about. Such people allow themselves to be vulnerable by being authentic and true to themselves. They are okay with letting go of the expectations of others in order to become exactly who they were made to be.

It's impossible to find happiness focusing on someone else's story. It's dangerous to compare your progress with the progress of others. The success of your journey in life should not be measured by the progress of others, but by your obedience to God in the things He has instructed you to do. God is focused on making us like Him—more like Jesus—not like other people. The Word tells us to be imitators of God (see Eph. 5:1). In turn, He will always show us who we are truly supposed to be.

As a pastor, I have found that it can be challenging not to compare myself with other pastors and ministries. I am often tempted to look at the great things other people, churches, and ministries are doing and say, "Why can't I do that?" Or even think, "Why are they getting that opportunity? I'm just as good and just as anointed as they are." But I have learned something extremely important: Do not focus on other people. Put the sole focus on God and serving Him. Focus on giving Him glory. I must serve the people God has placed in front of me.

You may not be called to minister to people from a stage, but your life has its own platform. Your significance is not based on having a certain number of social media followers or popularity. God has designed you to get the attention of those who need to be served by your gift. Whether you've been called to be a business owner, an educator, a politician, an electrician, an athlete, a health-care worker, or anything else at all, you can know that your gift comes with it's own form of prominence.

GOD'S BLUEPRINT

God's blueprint is the image He had in mind for you when He designed you. It's God's original thoughts, plans, and ideas about you. His original concept when creating you comes complete with the strategy necessary to maximize on your existence. God's blueprint gives you all the details you need to come into alignment with your destiny. This blueprint makes it possible for you to do what God has gifted you to do.

Once Adam sinned in the garden of Eden, our understanding of God's blueprint (and our self-image) was damaged. But when Christ came and died for us, we were reunited with God, and our original image was restored to God's original plan. The Bible says:

> *Death ruled like a king because Adam had sinned. But that cannot compare with what Jesus Christ has done. God has been so kind to us, and he has accepted us because of Jesus. And*

so we will live and rule like kings (Romans 5:17 CEV).

According to God's original blueprint, He designed us to rule this earth as His chosen authority, as adopted sons and daughters of God's royal family.

As we follow God's blueprint for portraying His image, we can follow the purpose blueprint for our lives. When we don't come into alignment with the image of who we are supposed to be, we'll have a hard time accepting God's plan for our lives. He has placed the future of what He wants to do in humanity within you.

I have found this revelation personally important. I had to accept some things about myself before God released me into another level of ministry and purpose. Until I understood who God has called me to be, as David Winston, I couldn't continue to advance higher. There is no way to get around that.

You have to know who God has made you to be. He hasn't made you somebody else. You don't have to ask or wonder why you are not like others—why you don't act, think, or speak like them. The Creator has deliberately selected your temperament. You are a never-before-seen original. He didn't miss anything, forget anything, or leave anything out. You are just the way He wanted you to be, and He will lead you to people, places, and resources that will help you become the best version of yourself. That's why it's important to follow God and adhere to the blueprint. He knows the training, encouragement, and correction that your potential requires. You have been made how you are, not just for your own sake, but for the benefit of others.

God has called you to do something great. But you will not do something great by leaving Him out of the equation. It doesn't happen that way, my friend. You have to team up with God. Together you are an unbeatable team. The team is not unbeatable because He teamed up with you, but because you teamed up with *Him*. You can't go wrong, wholeheartedly following God. Remember, God cannot mismanage your life. Trust Him, because He has the blueprint for your success.

EXERCISE: DAILY AFFIRMATIONS PRAYER

Say these affirmation declarations below out loud every day to transform your outlook on life and change your self-image.

- I am victorious in life, and everything that I put my hands to prospers.
- I am intelligent because I have the mind of Christ and godly wisdom.
- I am chosen and greatly loved by God.

- I am accepted and made perfect in God's eyes.
- I have been made wonderfully unique.
- I value who I am and what has been placed on the inside of me.
- I am strong, and I am powerful.
- I am free from fear, anxiety, and the opinions of others.
- I am blessing the world with the valuable resources that God has placed within me.
- I am a solution carrier and a walking distribution center for good.
- I am free to be everything that God has created me to be.
- I am God's best choice for the purpose and assignment He's given me.

CHAPTER 12

ATTRACTED BY YOUR AROMA

"Mmmmm…what are you wearing?" It's nice to get that positive reaction when you put on a new cologne or perfume. Some scents are so appealing that you feel the need to stop and ask the person for the name of the fragrance. On occasion, I will smell a perfume that smells so good that I will buy a bottle for my wife. Whenever she wears it, her scent makes me want to stay in close proximity to her. Her scent stimulates my behavior.

On the other hand, we have all experienced being around people who smell *really* bad. You don't want to be close to that person. You may find yourself trying to covertly create some distance between yourself and the smell. It reminds me of a cartoon I used to watch when I was a child. Looney Tunes had a character called Pepe Le Pew. Pepe was a French striped skunk who was constantly in search of love and adoration. The problem was, the females he tried to cozy up to would soon be repelled by his putrid odor. That's not really a surprise given the fact that he was a skunk. It was not necessarily who he was that was repelling the ladies, but the odor he was giving off.

This cartoon reminds me of some people. They can have all of the gifting, charisma, and skills, but if they don't have character, integrity, humility, kindness, and love working inside of them, eventually they will start to repel others with the stench of pride and selfishness. As we live our lives every day, we give off a vibe. It's almost like a scent or aroma meant to attract the right people, situations, and opportunities. *Your scent is your unique temperament.* As you release your *scent,* people will be drawn to you. The beauty is, some people won't even know why they're drawn to you. They just are. In the Bible, the apostle Paul writes:

> **As we live our lives every day, we give off a vibe. It's almost like a scent or aroma meant to attract the right people, situations, and opportunities.**

> *Now thanks be to God who always leads us in triumph in Christ, and through us diffuses the fragrance of His knowledge in every place. For we are to God the fragrance of Christ among those who are being saved and among those who are perishing* (2 Corinthians 2:14–15).

People should have a personal experience with God as a result of interacting with you. We are the ones who represent (or re-present) God to those who don't know Him. The fragrance of our love, our humility, our generosity, and our character speaks to others on God's behalf. The aroma of God's divine nature is in you and coming through you. The scripture says we are partakers of His divine nature (see 2 Pet. 1:4). We should reflect God's qualities. His nature should be part of your *personality* as you express your purpose in this world.

THE ESSENCE OF YOU

In my house, office, car, and bathroom, I am notorious for loving good smells and air fresheners. Candles, wall plug-ins, hand soaps—you name it, and I have it. Most people think it is my wife and laugh when they find out I am the one who likes home fragrances. Here's my confession: I shop at Bath & Body Works three times as much as my wife does. Now you know my secret. I like the good smells because of the calming effect they have on my senses and, subsequently, my mind. It's not something I control. It's more of a built-in function. Niki and I may differ sometimes in our scent preferences, but we both agree that we like when our house smells good.

Within the last decade, essential oils have become very popular. A few drops in a diffuser can fill the whole room with the fragrance. The oils are called *essential* because each of these oils are extracted from the essence of the plant. *Essence* is defined as "the quality of a thing that gives it its identity; or the intrinsic, indispensable properties of a thing."[1] In other words, these oils hold a very concentrated form of the exact elements that make them unique.

Many essential oil fragrances are manufactured in factories with high-tech equipment that can artificially produce synthetic compounds in mass quantities. However, two thousand years ago, that did not exist. They had to make fragrant oils the old-fashioned way. They would take aromatic plants like roses, for example, crush them, put them in oil, and heat the mixture. The oil would become infused with the essential substance of the plant. Once the oil was poured out, the house would be filled with the fragrance, just like when Mary took the very expensive fragrant oil and poured it out over Jesus' feet (see John 12:1–8). Imagine pouring a bottle of oil that cost a whole year's worth of paychecks on the feet of a man who is about to die. That's what Mary did.

Essential oil can represent you and who you are at the core. As you allow God to work through you, your specific fragrance is diffused into the atmosphere of society. As I mentioned before the scripture says we are God's fragrance being poured out among all people. That fragrance is meant to attract others. When this happens, people will start to be drawn to what you have.

It's not just about what you are doing or saying; it's about who you are. Your very *essence* draws them.

THE PROCESS OF THE OIL

In the Gospels, when it was time for Jesus to be captured, beaten, and sent to the cross, He asked Peter, James, and John to go with Him to the Garden of Gethsemane. This garden was essentially an olive orchard located near the Mount of Olives. Jesus went there to pray for strength for what He was about to endure, asking God if His assignment could be completed some other way—"Father, if it is Your will, take this cup away from Me…" (Luke 22:42). The scripture says He experienced such agony that He began to sweat great drops of blood. The pressure He must have felt in anticipation of unfathomable torture was immense. What happened to Jesus is a known rare condition called hematohidrosis, in which blood oozes from intact skin and can include sweating or crying blood.[2]

It is quite fitting that Jesus experienced this tremendous pressure, similar to the pressure that produces olive oil from olives, in an olive orchard. Olive oil in Jewish historical culture was used for many things—including for cooking, as fuel for fire, and as a topical treatment for skin aliments. Olive trees were known as one of the most durable trees around. They could survive fires, floods, and other kinds of damage and grow back unscathed.[3] They can also grow for more than one thousand years.[4]

The olive oil–making process involves five steps. First, the olive tree requires certain conditions. These trees are wind pollinated; therefore, it is hard for the olive tree to produce fruit without the strong winds of the east and refreshing winds of the west. Second, once the tree is pollinated and the olives are grown to proper maturity, the tree must be shaken to get the olives off. Third, the olive then has to be crushed until it is mush and no longer recognizable. Fourth, the mush must be pressed as much as possible. What comes out of this pressing is the very valuable oil. Fifth, and perhaps most important, is the separation. The oil must be strained and separated from any of the remaining remnants of the olive. Not until it's separated is it fit for use. I believe Jesus went through each of these steps as well, the last step being separation from the Father as He died on the cross for the sins of all humankind.

Perhaps you are in a season where you can identify with some of these elements. You are not going to the cross, but you may feel like life is pressing you so much that it's hard to recognize yourself anymore. Maybe you're being shaken, and circumstances have stolen the comforts of life. Perhaps the pandemic forced you to change, transition, or let go of something without even saying goodbye. Or you might be in the middle of a challenging situation with no end in sight. You feel the pressure and the pressing. Allow me to encourage you with this: Just as in the process of making olive oil, *when the pressing comes, something valuable will present itself.* Something valuable is about to be discovered, and it's coming out of you.

THE SCENT OF SACRIFICE

We are the fragrance that God is pouring out all over the world. We are the valuable oil that others need. The fragrant oil cannot be made without the crushing, which causes the essence of its elements to be exposed. Sometimes it can feel as though God is letting us go through difficult things or even pushing us toward difficult situations and seasons, but the force is necessary for the fragrance. The pressure is neces-

> **Sometimes it can feel as though God is letting us go through difficult things but the force is necessary for the fragrance.**

sary for the perfume. The very essence of who you were made to be is coming out, and it will attract a crowd. The Bible says, "Live a life filled with love, following the example of Christ. He loved us and offered himself as a sacrifice for us, a pleasing aroma to God" (Eph. 5:2 NLT). What Jesus did on the cross created a sweet-smelling aroma to God, but the aroma was created through Jesus' crucifixion, or *crushing*. The fragrant aroma of God's love for us manifested through Jesus' sacrifice.

At times, our will has to be broken so that the precious potential in us can be poured out of us. If you don't follow God past your own will, your potential will remain locked up in your heart and your greatness will never be manifested in the earth. If Jesus hadn't submitted His will to God by going to the cross, none of us could be called sons and daughters of God. When the time had come for Jesus to be arrested, He submitted His will to God saying, "…if it is possible, let this cup pass from me; nevertheless, not as I will, but as You will" (Matt. 26:39). *The time of great pressure will often require a great sacrifice.* Christ's example is one we should all follow.

Now let's connect this to your purpose. When you are successfully walking in your purpose and assignment, other people will ask, "How can I get what you have?" But as they get closer to you, the fragrance of your life should have them inquiring, "How can I be like you?" The difference between the two questions is important. The former is about achievement and attainment, but the latter represents quality, character, and personality. They want to get what you have—the joy, peace, fulfillment, kindness, love, prosperity, and confidence. People want that. Once people ask about your character and qualities, then you can point them back to the ultimate image consultant, Jesus.

Your life is constantly giving off an aroma. Your attitude dictates the aroma of your personality. Your character becomes your distinctive scent. Is your aroma repelling people or attracting people?

WEAR YOUR SCENT

Recently, I noticed a family friend was wearing a nice scent, and I asked her for the name so I could buy it for my wife. But when she told me the name of the fragrance, I recalled that my wife already owned that particular scent. However, it smelled different on our friend than it did on my wife. Every fragrance adapts to our natural body chemistry, so the fragrance instantaneously becomes unique to us.

Our different smells attract people in different ways. The aroma of your life will be able to attract and encourage somebody that I could never reach. I don't have a street-life testimony in which God saved me from a life of gangs and drugs. My life was shaped differently, and as a result, the aroma of my life and testimony may only attract certain people. Another person who has been saved by God's grace from the street life will have a different makeup to their experience and aroma. It will attract those who need to be encouraged by it. God wants to use your life as a sweet-smelling aroma to draw people to Him. And the beauty is, no two aromas are the same.

But there's a catch. People will only be attracted to Christ through you if you get close enough for them to pick up your scent. Don't isolate yourself. Take heart and be confident. Isolation usually comes from fear of rejection. You are a person of courage! Allow yourself to be around people so they can be encouraged by your life. Be confident in the aroma you are giving off. The right people will respond the right way to what they smell coming from your life.

EXERCISE: DEVELOPING YOUR SCENT

1.   List five single worlds that describe you (hyphenated words are okay too).

2.   Identify a few people that you respect and admire. They don't have to be people you know personally.

3.   For each person, list the three to five things that have drawn you to them. These are the reasons why you hold them in such high regard.

4.   Look at your list and identify the common, overlapping words and phrases that the people on your list share. Often the things that seem to regularly attract us to certain people represent qualities that we would like to display in our own lives.

5. Write those few words or phrases that the people have in common in capital letters at the bottom of the page. Confirm with God that these qualities are part of your unique calling.

THE JOURNEY OF PURPOSE

Get it together, David. Just breathe. Help me, Lord! Please! How will it look if I go out there all emotional like this? Those students are going to think I've committed some crazy sin, and my tears are filled with remorse. Tears were streaming down my face, I could barely stand. I was overcome with emotion. You would have thought I had just won the NBA Championship. It was like a flood I couldn't stop. I just couldn't believe it. A full-circle moment. Wow.

It was 2021, fall semester. I stood in the green room in the back of the chapel building on the campus of Oral Roberts University in Tulsa, Oklahoma. One by one, the praise and worship team prayed, ending in unison with a beautiful acapella song. But I was engulfed in my own moment, because I was about to speak to thousands of students at their biweekly chapel service. For them, it was just one of many services, but for me it was one of a kind. I've spoken at hundreds of services, big and small, so I was not being overcome with anxiety. But this service was very special for me. This service hit different.

Twenty minutes earlier, I had gone into the auditorium. *There it is, at the back corner,* I said to myself. I found the very seat I used to occupy as a freshman during my first year at ORU. Exactly eighteen years ago, almost to the day, I had sat in that very chapel building as an eighteen-year-old. During my freshman year, several weeks after the first semester had started, I remember a Friday morning chapel service similar to the one at which I was about to speak. I sat in that seat five rows from the back, and as the speaker began his sermon, I quietly said to myself, "I will never do that…ever." I was referring to preaching. I was adamant that full-time ministry was not in my future. As I sat there in denial, I was running away from my destiny.

Exactly eighteen years later, here I was—about to do what I said I would never do in the place I said I'd never do it. I've become what I said I would never become—a full-time minister of the gospel. And I couldn't be happier about it. I've been more fulfilled than I ever thought possible. Talk about a full circle moment. God certainly has a sense of humor. One thing is for sure, in order to be used by God to do great things, I had to develop the courage and confidence to be myself. I had to finally decide to stop running away.

EMBRACE YOUR YOU

Over the last decade, I have received one question more than any other: "How does it feel having to fill your father's shoes?" My answer is easy: I don't have to fill his shoes, because God didn't instruct me to do that. In reality, I could never fill my dad's shoes, because I am not him. God simply asks me to wear my own shoes while, continuing in my dad's footsteps to build upon the foundation he has already established. I get the honor of continuing the legacy of faith. That's my authentic journey—being myself while accomplishing what I was made for. What is your authentic journey? Is there a question that you are frequently asked?

The truth is, when we embrace who we are, we bring God glory. He is pleased, not only that we are living with authenticity, but that we trusted Him enough to be who He has purposed us to be. He is pleased because we had faith in His marvelous creation.

God doesn't accidentally choose people. He simply prepares the people He has already chosen. I want you to remember that you have been chosen. The Bible declares that even before God made the world, He chose us (see Eph. 1:4). This is your time to express what God has placed in your heart. The Bible also says, "...For there is a time there for every purpose and for every work" (Eccles. 3:17). I believe that time for you is now.

Purpose and personal growth don't function independently. *When personal growth stops, so does the journey of your purpose.* However, the more you understand your identity, the more you will see your destiny. If you become the person God created you to be, purpose many times will find you.

Your purpose is not coincidental. God created you and allowed you to be born because He saw that humankind needs your gift and purpose. It is a divine appointment for a role you are being asked to fill. You are going to be something and do something that people have not seen before. With all of the challenges that we face in our world—politically, culturally, economically, educationally, and so forth—God has raised you up to be a solution to one of *those* problems. You may be tempted to think that nobody needs you, but the truth is, the world can't do without you. Authenticity is always in high demand. Now it's time to purge your insecurities.

You might be asking yourself: *How will it happen? How will I know what to do? Where do I go from here?* As one of my favorite scriptures says, "Trust in the Lord with all your heart; do not depend on your own understanding. Seek His will in all you do and He will show you which path to take" (Prov. 3:5–6 NLT). My hope for you, as you have read this book, is not just that you would *change*, but that you would also become an *advocate* of change. Only changed people can change our communities, cities, nations, and society. As you mature and your greatness is realeased, others in your sphere of influence are blessed.

When your gift and purpose go missing from the earth, questions go unanswered, problems go unsolved, and humankind struggles to move forward. I believe our society is where it is right now, with all of the problems we are facing, because some people who were born to solve those problems refused to step up. They didn't choose to take a step of faith. They didn't step out. Instead they chose to step back, step down, or step away. Don't be like them. Take courage! The way you take courage is by living with authenticity.

Let God show you what to do next. He will give you the proper direction if you trust Him. Sometimes we get mad at God for not allowing us to take advantage of certain opportunities. We think we have missed those opportunities, but really God wants us to wait for *His* opportunity. When given the opportunity to be you, you cannot fail. On your journey,

> **When given the opportunity to be you, you cannot fail.**

it can be easy to get distracted. Comparison will work to cloud the clarity of God's calling on your life. And true individuality breeds significance. It all starts with being the authentic *you!*

Many people are waiting for permission to be themselves, but you are the only person who can give yourself that permission. When that permission is incorrectly delegated to others, you will get frustrated waiting on them. Insecurities will begin to gather past and present evidence to build a case against you and make you want to quit the journey. Stop waiting. Stop asking for permission to be yourself and just *be yourself*.

God will never give you a responsibility without giving you the ability. God will never give you a vision without making arrangements for the provision. However, the only way you can access it is by faith and trust in God.

God doesn't bless who you pretend to be. He blesses your authenticity, and He chose you to be here at this moment in history. He planted you where you are, and He wants your gift to be expressed on the earth. But it will only come about when you trust God.

As you look to move forward, focus on these four things:

1. Seek to gain understanding. Focus on correctly interpreting the passions and dreams that God has put in your heart.

2. Consider the responsibility you have to your purpose and assignment, and how it affects others.

3. Resolve in your heart to manifest everything God has put inside you. Make a courageous decision to be who you were designed to be by pursuing your purpose.

4. Develop a clear vision of the future. Even if it's something that might not happen for another twenty years, take time to close your eyes and see it. The clearer the vision, the faster the acceleration toward the known goal. Where do you want to go? Who do you want to be? What do you want to achieve? If you cannot see it, you cannot seize it.

This book is about the journey toward becoming who God has called you to become and doing what you were born to do. It's about appreciating our differences, casting off the opinions of others, and finding the authentic you. It's an encouragement to become your most confident self, developing the courage necessary to release your greatness.

You don't have to change who you are to be wanted. Honestly, no one can truly teach you how to be you. Books, tests, information, and people can give you insight for your journey. I hope that's what this book has done—given you insight and perspective. But God is the *only* one who can lead you on this journey. He's the only one who can dictate your destiny and prescribe your potential. Your Creator is the only one qualified to show you what it means to be authentically you.

ENDNOTES

Chapter 1—You Can Only Go as Far as Your Worth

1. T. D. Jakes, quoted in Steven Furtick, "How to Build Your Vision from the Ground Up | Q & A with Bishop T. D. Jakes," *YouTube*, (Oct. 26, 2017); www.youtube.com/watch?v=QVGk_jwyBXI.

Chapter 2—The Peculiar Package

1. *Strong's*, s.v. "Poiéma," Greek #4161; https://biblehub.com/greek/4161.htm.

2. Benjamin Elisha Sawe, "Famous Artwork: The Mona Lisa," *WorldAtlas* (July 26, 2017); https://www.worldatlas.com/articles/famous-artwork-the-mona-lisa.html.

3. Mariana Custodio, "The Mona Lisa: What Makes It a Masterpiece?" (Aug 3, 2021); https://marianacustodio.com/the-mona-lisa-what-makes-it-a-masterpiece.

4. Ibid.

5. A. Zelazko, "Why Is the Mona Lisa So Famous?" *Encyclopedia Britannica;* https://www.britannica .com/story/why-is-the-mona-lisa-so-famous.

6. Cash Luna, *In Honor of the Holy Spirit: He Is Someone, Not Something* (Miami, FL: Editorial Vida, 2012), 32.

Chapter 3—Just Be You and Win

1. Biz Carson, "This Is the True Story of How Mark Zuckerberg Founded Facebook, and It Wasn't to Find Girls," *Business Insider* (Feb. 28, 2016); https:// www.businessinsider.com/the-true-story-of-how -mark-zuckerberg-founded-facebook-2016-2.

2. Florence Littauer, *Personality Plus: How to Understand Others by Understanding Yourself* (Grand Rapids, MI: Revell, 2011), 15.

Chapter 4—Unlock Your Identity

1. *Strong's,* s.v. "Abram," Hebrew #87; https:// biblehub.com/hebrew/87.htm.

2. Craig Groeschel, "Overcomer Part 1— Overcoming the Curse of Comparing," *Life .Church,* YouTube (May 14, 2017); https://youtu .be/dE2W7kazyg4.

3. Joe Pierre, "Illusory Truth, Lies, and Political Propaganda: Part 1," *Psychology Today* (January 22, 2020); https://www.psychologytoday.com/us/blog/psych-unseen/202001/illusory-truth-lies-and-political-propaganda-part-1.

Chapter 5—Embrace Being the Underdog

1. Adam Clarke, *Adam Clarke's Commentary on the Bible* (1826). Public domain. https://biblehub.com/commentaries/clarke/1_samuel/17.htm.

2. *Strong's*, s.v. "Diakonia," Greek #1248; https://biblehub.com/greek/1248.htm.

3. DeVon Franklin, *The Hollywood Commandments: A Spiritual Guide to Secular Success* (New York: HarperOne, 2017).

4. Steve Gardner, "Six Kobe Bryant Quotes That Define NBA Legend's Career," *USA Today* (Jan. 26, 2020); https://www.usatoday.com/story/sports/nba/2020/01/26/kobe-bryant-death-six-quotes-define-nba-legends-career/4582571002/.

Chapter 6—Potential: Your Doorway to Greatness

1. Dr. Bob Rotella, *How Champions Think: In Sports and in Life* (New York: Simon & Schuster, 2015), 6–10.

2. *Strong's,* s.v. "Elohim," Hebrew #430; https:// biblehub.com/hebrew/430.htm.

3. Bill Winston, *Revelation of Royalty: Rediscovering Your Royal Identity in Christ* (Lake Mary, FL: Charisma House, 2021), 193.

4. *Strong's,* s.v. "Abad," Hebrew #5647; https:// biblehub.com/hebrew/5647.htm.

5. Bill Winston, *Faith & the Marketplace* (Oak Park, IL: Bill Winston Ministries, 2016), 110.

Chapter 7—No Small Thinkers Allowed

1. Joel Osteen, *Your Best Life Now: 7 Steps to Living at Your Full Potential* (FaithWords, 2015), 11–12.

Chapter 10—Courage: The Power to Be Transparent

1. *Merriam-Webster Dictionary,* s.v. "Courage"; https://www.merriam-webster.com/dictionary/ -age#etymology. *Online Etemology Dictionary,* s.v. "Courage"; https://www.etymonline.com/word/ courage.

2. Brené Brown, "The Power of Vulnerability," *TED* (2011); https://www.ted.com/talks/brene_brown _the_power_of_vulnerability.

3. Judy Scheel, "Perfectionism: Inherited or A Psychological Solution?" *Psychology Today* (Apr. 18,

2015); https://www.psychologytoday.com/us/blog/when-food-is-family/201504/perfectionism-inherited-or-psychological-solution.

4. *Merriam-Webster,* s.v. "Paralysis"; https://www.merriam-webster.com/dictionary/paralysis.

5. Quoted in Rachel Montanez, "21 Motivational Quotes for Your Job Search or Career Change," *Forbes Magazine* (Aug. 20, 2019); www.forbes.com/sites/rachelmontanez/2019/08/19/21-motivational-quotes-for-your-job-search-or-career-change/#562a78dd2630.

Chapter 11—Don't Dare Compare: Maintaining Your Value

1. "Prestigious Placement - Neil Harris' Testimony," *Bill Winston Ministries* (Dec. 19, 2019); https://vimeo.com/215079918.

2. Joel Osteen, *Your Best Life Now: 7 Steps to Living at Your Full Potential* (FaithWords, 2015), 59, 104.

Chapter 12—Attracted by Your Aroma

1. *American Heritage® Dictionary of the English Language, Fifth Edition,* s.v. "Essence"; https://www.thefreedictionary.com/essence.

2. "NIH GARD Information: Hematohidrosis," NORD (National Organization for Rare Disorders); https://rarediseases.org/gard-rare-disease/hematohidrosis.

3. Cátia Brito, et al, "Drought Stress Effects and Olive Tree Acclimation under a Changing Climate," Plants (July 17, 2019), National Library of Medicine; https://www.ncbi.nlm.nih.gov/pmc/articles/PMC6681365/.

4. Miquel Ros, "Spain's Ancient Olive Trees: New Taste for Old Flavor," CNN (Jan. 24, 2017); https://www.cnn.com/travel/article/millenary-olive-trees-spain/index.html.

ABOUT DAVID S. WINSTON

David S. Winston serves as a pastor at Living Word Christian Center in Forest Park, Illinois, under his father and Senior Pastor Dr. Bill Winston. Additionally, he serves as the international director of Bill Winston Ministries. David is also the founder and creator of the Winston Leadership Institute, preparing next generation leaders to better society by leading God's way.